Turnaround Summer

How Real Men Launched
a Lost Boy into Manhood

Paul Hansen

Book Publishers Network
P.O. Box 2256
Bothell • WA • 98041
PH • 425-483-3040
www.bookpublishersnetwork.com

Copyright © 2009 by Paul Hansen

All rights reserved. No part of this book may be reproduced, stored in, or introduced into a retrieval system, or transmitted in any form, or by any means (electronic, mechanical, photocopying, recording, or otherwise) without the prior written permission of the publisher.

10 9 8 7 6 5 4 3 2 1

Printed in the United States of America

LCCN 2009906715
ISBN10 1-935359-17-7
ISBN13 978-1-935359-17-3

Cover Photography: Linda Hansen
Editor: Julie Scandora
Cover Designer: Laura Zugzda
Typographer: Stephanie Martindale

I dedicate this book:

First, to my father, who despite adversity never lost sight of me and never gave up on me;

Second, to all the fathers and sons who have been troubled by their inability to connect;

Third, to the sons who will one day have sons of their own and have the opportunity to break the chain of fatherly neglect.

Contents

Foreword. vii
Preface ix
Acknowledgements. xiii
Introduction. xv
It All Started Here. 1
Another First for Everyone. 15
That Summer 33
Those Giant Rainbow Trout 43
What Crisis?. 51
First Pack Trip. 59
More Hay!. 83
Murtle Lake 89
Back Home on the Farm 115
In Pursuit of the GIANT TROUT. 123
The Journey Back Home 135
Reflections. 141
Epilogue 145
If 151

Forward

Paul Hansen gives us a field day away from the mundane in *Turnaround Summer*. He sends us on a journey back into the adolescence that most men wish they had lived. And his tales of desire and initiation capture your heart and keep you on the edge of your seat.

Every man can identify with the longing for initiation into manhood. Deep in every man's heart, he knows that he was made to "arrive," to "show up," to "rise" to the occasion. Every man longs to have a strength to offer to those he loves and to the world. But most men wonder, "If I did step into the situation, if I did try to make a difference … would I be able to? Do I have what is needed here?

On the other side of the coin, every man secretly fears that when the test comes, when push comes to shove, ultimately, he will crumble and appear weak. The only thing that changes this for a man is initiation by another man, usually his father, teaching him who he really is, what he has, what he's made of.

Not so long ago, young men received rites of passage by their fathers, or maybe a grandfather or an uncle. A young man longs for his strength to be called up and tested. He remembers landmark events in his youth, such as his father teaching him to shoot a rifle, catch a fish, spend the night in the woods, deal with a bully, or even drive a car. And from these moments a young man derives his confidence that he is what every boy knows the world expects and needs him to be—a man.

Unfortunately, the days where fathers understood the importance of providing these masculine rites of passage are all but gone. Television, computers, and gaming platforms have replaced packs, horses, fishing rods, and compasses. Masculine initiation is an art form that has gone out of vogue in our American culture, and it's left us with a generation of men who are in deep identity crisis. A whole crop of men today do not know how to catch a fish, repair a broken pipe, fix the lawn mower, talk to their wives, engage in a meaningful conversation with their teenage son or daughter, or be a man of integrity—a man of character, an honest man, a good man. Why? Because they were never shown how.

But every man, deep down, wants those things, even if he's turned his back on them and pretends he doesn't because he knows they add up to what it means to be a true man. That's what *Turnaround Summer* is about.

Paul Hansen reminds us of days gone by. Where values were different and boys were taught by older men the deep lessons that a boy *needs* to learn, lessons that show him what he is made of and who he is on the inside and how to deal with fear.

Paul is a master storyteller, and through vivid and exciting tales of his experiences on a ranch in Canada, he weaves together a template for what every young man needs and what every father must understand about fathering.

Randy Lawrence
Pastor of Adventure Community Church
Duvall, WA

Preface

Father. This word gets any number of reactions, stirs up memories too numerous to list, takes on an array of physical descriptions but always describes a particular individual in each and every one of our lives. Like it or not, we all have or had one, whether known or unknown.

Some people got the family and father that dreams are made of—loving, helpful, a guiding force, inspirational, spiritual, a loving husband to your mother, and always available when needed.

A lot of us got that with a few missing pieces. And the gaps culminated over the years as wounds on our hearts. John Eldredge, author of *Wild at Heart* and *Way of the Wild Heart*, has written extensively on wounded hearts and how to heal them. Many people claim to have it all together but are suffering inside. Then they find the opportunity to open up to someone and share their story of what lies deep within, and the healing begins. I was on a men's retreat one time, and two of the men in our group, outwardly very composed and stable, seemed to be drawing closer to the realization that their hearts were troubled. As the days went by, they found themselves feeling the strength and compassion of the men they were with, and felt safe sharing their stories of neglect and abuse at the hand of their fathers. Thus began their healing.

We can have this kind of experience only if we accept that the wounds on our hearts are not our fault, were not solicited by us, and were perpetrated by a person who perhaps had the same experience in his life. The idea is to allow healing in our hearts and break the cycle of neglect or abuse.

I have known men who outwardly demonstrated a sort of apathy about their sons or daughters. If you could look back in a time machine, you would probably find that that way of relating to the children had gone on for generations. Maybe the neglect was not by choice but due to economic hard times, a sick or dying father who left prematurely, or a father that lacked communication skills. Someone suffered the loss of either the father's time or his lack of even temperament, focus, or judgment. That absence filtered into his fathering skills without anyone realizing it, and there it remained for him to pass along to the next generation.

So what is the solution? Is there a way out of the circle of neglect? Can we change what appears to be our destiny? I believe we can break the cycle if we recognize the wounds we carry, understand how they came about, and decide to act differently, with love rather than fear and pain in our hearts.

I had a childhood that involved a father who loved me dearly and would have probably done things a lot differently had he known that his heart was troubled from the wounds he had suffered when his father died before he was twelve. Left to help his mother raise his brother and sisters, Dad pursued success with almost a vengeance. When he and my mother married, he was still trying to right the wrong of poverty and become a self-made man. As a boy, I admired his success and his carefully chosen words. But I missed the closeness of a father-son relationship with a supportive mother and harmony

Preface

amongst brothers and sisters. Again, it wasn't Dad's fault that his father had passed away so early in his life and he had to help support the family, but taking on that responsibility at such an early age left him frustrated and fearful of failure.

So what I got from this was a loving father, parents who divorced over issues that never got resolved, and wounds on my heart about love, marriage, and being a father to my sons. After sixty years, I read a lot of John Eldredge's works, finally connected with my wounds, and at last discovered some of what my dad had been trying to say to me. He felt sad for the mess the family situation had made on us children, yet he strived in the midst of it to make good on what he could. That summer was one such effort on his part, his gift of an adventure to take me into manhood, which would also instill in me responsibility, a work ethic, and the strength to leave home without regret.

This story is for men who have missed the childhood experience, that they may take up the sword of victory and create a positive experience with the boys in their lives, whether they be their own sons or nephews, grandsons, neighbors, friends, or players on the Little League team. It is never too late. During the summer of my fifteenth year, my father made sure that I received an experience that launched me into the start of manhood. He could not directly provide it to me so he entrusted another man, one in whom he had the utmost respect and confidence, to mentor me.

Every boy needs an adventure in his youth. Any man can provide this to any boy, when the conditions are right. Ted Helset was that man to the boy Paul Hansen. But the experience has so much more power when it comes from his own father.

I encourage every man to look within his heart and see if there are wounds that could be limiting his ability to be the loving, compassionate father his son needs. Heal them now and allow a deeper relationship to form. Enter into your son's life and make that indelible mark on his heart that he will cherish forever. Do it now.

Acknowledgements

I thank all the people that contributed to this book:

My wife, Linda, who heard the stories time and time again and suggested I write a book about my adventures and share them with all my friends.

My three sons, who drew from some of my experiences by being dragged bodily from their sleep to go pursue the elusive fish at all hours of the morning.

My dad, who engineered the adventure to Canada for me. I know he's up there telling anybody that will listen how it turned out.

My mother, who put up with all of my trip. I bless her for being so patient with me.

Ted, Jennie, Clara, Roy, Jim, Ellen, Harold, all of the extended family, and friends in the neighborhood. You all share in this story; it was you that made it happen.

The friends and family who read the rough manuscript and inspired me to pursue it further.

To the editor, Julie Scandora, who patiently corrected the messes I made of structure and punctuation and kept me on target.

To the publisher, Sheryn Hara, who saw an engaging story and encouraged me to publish it.

Introduction

Within each of us is a memory of a time and place that we particularly cherish, an event, perhaps, that changed our lives for the better. From such an event, I draw to tell of a summer that lives on and on in my memory—a true adventure, a period of growing up, and a fond look back at what was the biggest out-of-family experience of my life.

The story takes place on a farm in British Columbia, north of the town of Clearwater at the south end of Wells Gray Provincial Park. It involves a family that took me in for a summer and their neighbors and other acquaintances. I went to this place with expectation, curiosity, and reservation. My summer with the neighborhood kids was being disrupted, for sure. Who would I play kick the can with? Ride with me on bikes to the bakery? Join me in some kind of mischief?

Little did I know that this summer would blossom into an experience that still rings clear. So profoundly did it affect me—throughout my life—that I must share it with you. I want you to know how the past can give way to a better life and, most important, how much boys need men to look up to, emulate, and guide them.

It All Started Here

School was not out yet, April 1961, and the looming question in my mind was what would the summer bring. I certainly wasn't wild about classes for another six weeks, so I needed a game plan to carry me through.

Dad had been talking about a drive up to where he used to go hunting and fishing in Canada. It sounded like a good idea.

As a small boy of six to ten, I would wait for him to come home from those two-week fishing or hunting trips (or both if luck and the gods wished it) to welcome his whiskered face and a strange peculiar odor that lurked around him. Excitement surrounded his arrival as I discovered what he had dispatched to an untimely end and whether we would eat it or it would hang on the wall to scare the life right out of us kids.

The prospect, however, of a trip to that strange uncharted wilderness to the north had an alluring effect on me, so I agreed that we should pursue the idea. Dad proceeded by writing a letter to the Helsets, the owners of the place of his visits, and we waited for a reply.

In June, I would turn fifteen, already feeling as if I'd survived adulthood. My parents' marriage of twenty-seven years had halted abruptly in an ugly divorce. It seemed to me that I was the coveted prize in the whole scheme of things. Of course, I was seeing that through my own eyes. I was subpoenaed to appear in the court for one day of the trial by my father's attorney to testify against my own mother. The judge was outraged that I had been brought between my parents as a witness and refused to have my testimony. Not having a way to get me back to school, he came up with a solution for my "day in court." He assigned his clerk the task of finding something for me to do the rest of the day, so he gave me a list of tasteful trials to watch. One murder trial was especially interesting! As usual, no one in our family won anything from this. However, my mother was awarded custody of me.

In the early years of my life, our family did a lot of vacationing in the summer. We would all pile in the station wagon and head to some really nice resort or cabin by the water. We went to Priest Lake, Idaho, one year and stayed in a cabin on the lake. I remember being immersed in the water that recently had had six inches of ice on it, probably melted a few days before we got there. My sister, Sally, brother, Carl, and I filled our time emptying the lake of fish and hunting giant toads and bullfrogs. At the end of the stay, it had been decided that my mother, sister, and I would fly home from Spokane. Dad and Carl would travel on for their own adventure. This presented a problem in that the frog I had exiled to a shoebox had to go home on the plane. Elaborate attempts to relieve me of custody of the frog failed, and we were off to the airport. Where the parents had failed, the airline authorities prevailed. The stewardess convinced me the frog did not like flying, and I think she said it might even die. So Froggy was put in her charge to be returned to the wild. (This frog had huge legs, and I wondered if he ever made it back to the lake.)

It All Started Here

Another summer we spent at a resort on Hood Canal, west of Seattle. This again involved water, which rarely froze because of its high salt content. The thermal experience, however, was the same. By this time in my life, I was immune to the cold water, so swimming in water of any temperature was high on the fun scale. Again, fish were in abundance, caught in the morning, put in a pail of water to live out the rest of their lives, which was about noon. The fish fairy came in the night and hustled them off to who-know-where.

Up from the beach was a beautiful lawn, accented with a stream, waterfall, and pond filled with GIANT RAINBOW TROUT! It didn't take long for my new-found camp friend and me to cook up a plan. We got at least one onto the lawn before someone spotted us, followed by a lot of yelling and finger-pointing.

All of the family vacations involved adventure, a sense of togetherness, and a great deal of fun. Well, usually.

Some ended up in disaster, such as the time my brother ordered me to try and attack him and he would defend himself with his hand-to-hand combat he had been learning. This was the night before we were going to Mt. Rainier for a few days as a family outing. I begged to bow out, but he threatened to slug me if I didn't attack. I lunged, he flipped me over his shoulder, and I screamed for probably two hours while dad interrogated the both of us.

"He's got a bump on his shoulder; he's fine," Dad declared.

But Mom thought it should be looked at. She was out-voted.

Two days later, we returned from the trip, having not made the hike up to the snow line due to the pain I was in. I felt as though it was my fault because, as Mom had put it, "He doesn't feel good, Ben. We need to have him looked at!" The doctor set my broken collarbone while Mom and Dad looked on in silence. Dad took us all out to dinner later. Four of us all had hamburgers; he had the broiled crow.

Three weeks had passed since Dad had sent the letter to his friend Ted in Canada. I began to wonder if the pony express went that far into the woods. And what about grizzly bears, Indians, insufficient postage? With the delay, I got excited and worried that the trip might not happen. In anticipation of the worst, we made contingency plans, possibly ship me out for the summer on someone's big yacht as a deckhand and general laborer. I thought the idea of companionship for a teenage daughter would be a good idea, but Dad thought my summer should be a working experience. We sent letters to all sorts of yacht brokers, yacht clubs, yacht repair yards. No one got the idea, thought I just wanted a free ride. Having not heard back, I occupied my time by tying flies and looking through the photo albums of Dad's trips from years past. A definite sense of adventure came through in the pictures—rugged situations, riders on horseback, successful game hunts, and most of all, GIANT RAINBOW TROUT!

My first impression of the latter was that I wasn't tying flies on big enough hooks. Salmon would have been a better definition of what the pictures showed, given their size. They couldn't be trout.

Then one Saturday morning, Dad stopped by the house, and we went outside to visit.

"This came in my mail yesterday. I think you'd like to look at it."

It was postmarked Clearwater, British Columbia.

It All Started Here

Ted Helset Guiding Service

Clearwater British Columbia

Dear Ben,

It's good to hear from you. It's been awhile since you were up to hunt and fish. I always enjoy having you and Walt up for a couple of weeks. Things are good at this end. Winter is gone, and the guide season will be starting soon. I have been out on my trap lines throughout the winter and am looking forward to some warmer weather. Jennie and the family are fine; the children are ready to get back outside and enjoy the sun.

A summer up here for your son sounds like it might work. I can always use an extra pair of hands. He sounds like a hard worker. I hope he isn't shy about pitching in with all there is to do. We don't have an extra bedroom, but he might enjoy sleeping out on the covered porch. We'll tie a piece of firewood to his leg so the mosquitoes don't fly off with him in the night.

Write me back soon, and tell me when you would be coming up, I will save a portion of the woodpile for him to entertain himself with.

I would like to have you get a couple of parts for an old muzzle loader that I'm trying to restore. I think Warshall's in Seattle has what I need. I will send you a description in my next letter. Also when you come up, feel free to stay for a while if you like—lots of fish in Hemp Creek.

We will be starting hay season so your son will be plenty busy soon as he gets here.

Will be waiting to hear back from you soon. Tell Paul we look forward to meeting him; he should have a busy summer and maybe get in some good fishing along the way. I hope he is comfortable around the horses; lots to do there, also.

Take care. Looking forward to seeing you.

Sincerely,

Ted. Helset

Comfortable around horses! Mosquitoes that carry you away! Haying season! I thought you bought it in bales at the feed store. But the part about fishing sounded like the height of the trip. I'd need to start tying more flies. I couldn't believe he'd written back. I was so wired about the trip. I couldn't wait to tell all my friends.

"Dad, do you think we should start getting our gear together?"

"You need to finish school first. Concentrate on that; there's plenty of time to pack. I need to talk with your mom. She has to give this a go first."

I doubted she'd block this, a chance for her to have a little peace and quiet in the house. And for me, a whole summer on a ranch with horses, hay, GIANT TROUT, and whatever else they had to offer, which wouldn't be anything like around home. Kind of like scout camp, for grownups, but no uniforms. I wondered if anyone else lived in the area near them; someone my age would have been too much to ask.

By mid-June, we were pretty much ready to go. I had received a new fly pole and reel for my birthday, feathers and stuff, and a really short haircut for the summer. I had all my stuff packed in an old Army duffle bag, fishing gear, and a rather inexpensive hunting knife. The knife, of course, was to do battle with the famous Canadian man-eating bears and cats. No self-respecting bear or cat was going to mess with the crew-cut kid from Seattle. Shortly thereafter, we set out for the North Country.

The drive from Seattle to Clearwater station is about four hundred and some miles. We would do it in less than three days, stopping twice overnight. For the last time, our little traveling friend would accompany us on the road. He was a rather awkward bird of great size who, when I was a child, would fly alongside and above the car on long trips. We named him Beeper as he made noises quite similar to a honking car horn. He was always waiting on the utility pole outside our house, slept on a pole near our accommodations when we stayed the night in a distant town, and returned to the pole at our house when we came back. He would disappear from sight in between trips, as he was only a traveling companion. He did have one flaw, which always caused excitement—unscrewing the wire insulators on the poles and throwing them at the car. Of course, Dad would swerve the car on those occasions to avoid a broken windshield, and lots of hollering would ensue.

So Dad, I, and of course, Beeper, who showed up late (met us near the border), stopped in Chilliwack the first night. The following day we proceeded north to Kamloops. On the way, we traveled through Hope, which in a few years would see a devastating landside with fatalities. Kamloops is kind of the jumping-off point into the Canadian wilderness. In the early sixties, everything from there on up was pretty rugged, but oh so beautiful.

More than just pretty scenery affected me. The drive out also released me from the bonds of city life, my neighborhood and friends, Seattle, and a lot of extra baggage that needed to stay home. Some photos of hunting trips five to ten years in the past kept flashing into my thoughts. There was Dad, his good friend Walt, and of course, none other than the mysterious Ted Helset. Dad had always spoken fondly of Ted. Few people in my father's eye stood as prominently as he in character and content. Dad had a criteria of sorts by which all men were measured; few made the cut. Women had it even harder. In the years before Dad's death, he added one to his short list, my wife of thirty-some years, Linda.

Dad had told me in the weeks before more about Ted's family, the farm, and the area. Ted and his wife, Jennie, had five children: the oldest, Clara, followed by Roy, Jim, Ellen, and Harold. Clara and her husband lived at the entrance to Wells Gray Provincial Park and were employed by the park service. Roy and his wife lived across the north field in a place of their own. Jim, Ellen, and Harold lived at home. I didn't know how old they were then, but I did know that Roy guided with his dad.

We arrived in Clearwater. The town didn't have a whole lot in the sixties. We stopped and picked up the usual—flour, salt pork, bear traps, gunpowder, coffee, a really big knife, and a small pistol for shooting mosquitoes. Actually, that was all on the list in my head. We only had lunch there, got a couple of candy bars, and headed about twenty-five miles up the road to the Helsets'. We traveled on a gravel road from Clearwater to the farm and passed a number of other farms along the way. I marveled at the tenacity of people living way up in those parts had to have, hard working people who, out of love of nature or a sense of adventure, had come that way. They hadn't bailed out of society; they worked hard and raised sons and daughters who trekked off to universities and came back with the education to make a difference in that rugged wilderness.

I knew that I was going to be in different company than I was used to, and I just wasn't sure that I'd fit in.

As we traveled up the gravel road, we said good-bye to Beeper, no more utility poles up there with the glass knobs for him to throw. I decided that was a good place for him to stay. I thought he'd be good company for some other boy traveling the other direction back to the city. He'd been a good traveling companion, but I needed to be on my own now. That is, unless Ted Helset had a bird that traveled with him on horseback, throwing pine cones, and then I might reconsider…

The trip up was nearly at its end. Dad pointed out familiar landmarks and places he recognized.

"Paul, there's Hemp Creek that flows through the Helsets'. I've caught trout in there before while we were waiting to get out on a trip."

I was climbing into Dad's lap, trying to get a glimpse out the left side of the car. He wove back and forth across the gravel road, and I thought that might be the premature end right there. I could see a clearing on my left coming up and some buildings. Nothing too spectacular, but something told me that was it. The road turned left, and over a bridge, two cabins on the left, and beyond that a larger white house, various outbuildings, and a hitching post. We pulled up to the white house. Two small children in the front yard looked as puzzled as I felt, and Mrs. Helset came out the front door and waved.

"Hello, Mr. Hansen. So good to see you. And this must be Paul. Did you have a good trip up?"

Dad took the lead, which in social circles was always his forte. It was just as well; someone had stapled my mouth shut for the moment. I was sure it would open back up soon, though. Mrs. Helset carried a little baby, Harold, I assumed at the moment. She introduced me to The Two, Jim and Ellen. Jim

Jennie Helset Jim and Ellen probably 1959

was a slender boy, very polite and soon warmed up. I think he had my summer all planned out that minute. Ellen was a little cutie; she just looked at me and smiled a lot. I decided then and there that we should be good friends. She was not going to leave my side, nor was Jim, for any long period of time, unless Mom locked them in the attic!

"Ted will be back tomorrow, out with a fishing party. He's been gone for four days but very anxious to get back to see the both of you."

That news came as a bit of a disappointment—another day waiting to meet *the* man.

"You and Paul can put your things in the small cabin, then come on up for supper here at the house."

As we drove back down to the little cabin, I admired all the horses in the north pasture and the small home up on the hill ahead to my left. Perhaps that was Roy and his wife's place. I wanted to go dangle a line in Hemp Creek, the unpacking could wait.

The early fishing did not materialize. Dad was plenty tired from the drive up, so we just got settled and soon headed up to the farmhouse for my first experience in farm-style cooking. It's no different from city cooking; the portions are just somewhat larger. More on this later, like the twenty-one pancakes I ate one morning.

Mrs. Helset (hereafter referred to by her first name, Jennie) and her daughter-in-law, Roy's wife, Marlene, had put together a nice supper of fried chicken, tons of vegetables, dessert of pie with whipped cream, and farm-fresh milk that was served in a pitcher. It had the consistency of half and half, cold, comforting, and very satisfying. I think of that milk now, every time I put a glass of one percent to my lips…

All that time before, during, and after the meal, The Two just stared at me. By that time, I had warmed up to the situation and started to communicate with all present. I was not what you would call a silent child; social reserve came to me later. As I participate in the conversation, The Two entered in and started to ask questions of me and tell me a lot about the farm. As the evening progressed, we all exchanged tidbits about ourselves and shared some little stories. Soon Dad showed signs of the long trip, and the conversation changed to what time breakfast was prepared. *SIX O'CLOCK? Are we going fishing or what?* I usually didn't open an eye till at least seven. They had to get up about four thirty or five. I'd be curious to see how long they could keep that up. *What a joke.*

So off to bed I went. The bunk bed was a welcome place after such a busy day. The air was quiet outside with only a few farm sounds and off in the distance sounds from the woods—occasional cracking of branches, strange noises, and what must have been a very large dog howling in the night. *Except there are no dogs in the woods. I don't think there are any wolves up there, just couldn't be…* (Wrong again pal!)

The sun was not even up much less a trace of daylight showing when my feet hit the floor. In the north, you don't wake to balmy temperatures, not even close. Setting your bed on fire might even be a good idea if you're fond of the warmth. Breakfast was another meal of enormous proportions. I had consumed coffee on several occasions prior, but not like that. Their brew was man's coffee, stand a spoon in it, use it to degrease an automobile engine, disinfect a bad wound, multipurpose stuff. It was great, and you were wide awake in about five minutes, so no problem with the time of day. Cooking and caring for all that there was to do at home took up all of Jennie's time. She was a tireless woman, yet seemed to have a love of all she did. I never saw her angry but for a few times.

Dad and I and The Two headed down to Hemp Creek after the sun came up, and I got my first taste of fishing on

It All Started Here

Paul and Jim, Hemp Creek
2006

the creek. Being the self-proclaimed fisherman that I was, I choose to dispatch those brutes from the creek with a fly, tied by me, of course. The first few casts ended up in some misplaced willow branches, which produced peals of laughter from Jim and Ellen.

"Just put a worm on your hook; they love 'em," Jim suggested.

I was not going to be reduced to such mundane methods. Finally I got a good cast, and a good sized brook trout grabbed it. There was not much fighting room, so I had to get him in quick. Dad was down the creek a bit and having equal luck with small spinners and spoons. The trout actually were so active you could have used a soda pop cap and a bent safety pin. Having caught enough for dinner and dinnertime approaching ("lunch" in the city), we headed up and out of Hemp Creek. As we walked toward the house, a string of horses and riders came down the road from the north. Led by a gentleman on horseback, wearing a beat-up, medium color, brimmed hat, dark trousers, suspenders, and a blue work shirt. It had to be Ted Helset.

Another First for Everyone

Jim and Ellen squealed with excitement and took off running for the farmhouse.

Dad exclaimed, "Well, would you look at that. The fishermen return!"

I stood there for a moment, taking in the scene that was unfolding before my eyes: four very dusty, smiling horseback riders and a couple of kids running to greet them. The music was the only element missing, what with Jennie standing on the porch, apron and all.

Dad politely exclaimed, "Paul, why don't we go to our cabin, clean these fish, and have a bite of lunch while the folks get settled? We'll go over later, visit with Ted, and catch up on things."

I really couldn't argue with his logic, even though I was as curious as a cat. All this preparation, and another delay! I resigned myself peacefully to the task of cleaning those beautiful trout and peeking over at the activity of packs being offloaded, saddles removed, and all else that takes place at the end of a journey.

We entertained ourselves for the time being with eating our lunch. I pawed around in my gear, making sure I hadn't forgotten anything, as if it mattered. It was twenty-five miles back to Clearwater, and the town didn't exactly have a Cabella's, or a Sears. I was sure that something was missing. *But deal with it, Paul. It's all going to work out.*

Dad and I talked about his trips previous up there, as we had for weeks prior. He told me about catching his big trout and the birch saplings he had cut for a frame he had made to mount the fish on. That fish and frame still adorn the wall of our cabin in the mountains of Washington, along with his moose and deer mountings. Even then, I admired Dad's enthusiasm for adventure and going out of his way to make things happen. I share that focus today. As he would say, "Nothing ventured, nothing gained."

Just shortly before supper, Dad and I sat on the front porch. I aimlessly whittled on a piece of tree branch, knowing I'd have nothing more than a pile of shavings on the porch, being as I couldn't concentrate and I wasn't really that creative with a knife. Other than carving my initials on things I probably shouldn't have, I just loved the feel of a sharp knife, working its way through a piece of forgiving wood. Looking up the road, I spotted Ted come out of the farmhouse and turn down the road, heading for our cabin. He was obviously all cleaned up, shaven and hair slicked back, ready for action. My heart suddenly stopped beating.

Silence.

Dad and I stepped out into the front of the cabin, and Ted welcomed Dad to the farm.

Now let's take a little time here, while the two men exchange greetings, share a little mild profanity, and talk up the fishing.

I didn't know how tall the man was, but let's just say he seemed big. He was born in Norway in February 1910, Torbjorn Nilsen Helseth, one among five brothers and four sisters.

His family had a large farm, so he was obviously not allergic to work from the beginning. Ted and a friend sailed to Canada in the spring of 1930 and worked on a grain farm in Saskatchewan. By 1933, he had traveled to Blue River, British Columbia, having decided not to go back to Norway for the time, thus missing a two-year whaling expedition on his uncle's boat. In Blue River, he met the lovely Ruth Jennie Viola Munter. A year later, February 1934, they married and, in the ensuing twenty-five years, had five children.

Back to 1961. Ted turned his attention to me and offered out his hand.

"Hello, Paul. I am pleased to meet you."

He had a very clear speaking voice, well understood, and a nice touch of Norwegian accent. The handshake had been softened for my benefit, and to avoid potential injury. That man had hands that could have crushed a bowling ball. Years of hard work, never backing away from a physical task, and taking on some jobs he probably should have had help with left him in the peak of health for a man of some fifty years. Ted took both of my hands and carefully examined them.

"Vell, they von't look like that at the end of the summer!"

I suspected he knew a great deal upon which to base those kinds of predictions. I'd be happy just to return with fingers still sprouting out of them. Questions followed.

"Do you think you can help vith the haying? It's pretty hard vork."

His accent, pronouncing the Ws as Vs captivated me, and the foreignness only lent more mystery to my image of the man.

"I'm sure going to try, Mr. Helset. Do you work all day?"

"Ve start about five o'clock while it is nice and cool and break for dinner about eleven. Then back in the field at about four till about dusk. Ve take the noontime off ven it's hot and do other things."

Like split wood, I'll bet, or dig ditches.

Actually the noon hour turned out to be blessed—supper and a short nap, time to poke around the farm, maybe go for a swim in the creek, or shoot something!

After further discussion, we all retired to the farmhouse where, once again, Jennie had outdone herself cooking the supper meal. That was the first time I met Francis, a hired hand who worked on the farm. He was quiet to me at first, but that finally dissolved with my mindless chatter constantly bombarding him. Table discussion was always at machine-gun level if the day had not taken its toll on us. Of course, my attention focused on listening to the stories told by Ted and watching Jennie's eyes either in excitement or some degree of regret. The dear woman had seen her share of very hard work, mixed in with great accomplishments and an occasional disaster, just to keep the load in balance. Dad took all the interaction in with a smug grin on his face; he knew my stay was going to be good for me.

"Paul, have the children shown you around the farm yet?"

"No, Mr. Helset, just the creek, where we caught trout this morning."

"Those little trout von't fill the frying pan. Ve need to take you up to Stillvater, and catch some man-sized trout!"

Once again, my heart quit beating.

After supper, we retired to the living room/parlor, and Ted and Dad got into a deep discussion about trips past. The Two plus myself stayed glued to their sharing of adventures and times gone by. Dad told about the time he couldn't get his little Winchester pump 22 to sight in.

"I fiddled with the two adjustments on the rear sight, tried it, and still off. I kept adjusting and retesting. Bullets hitting

Another First for Everyone 19

everywhere but the tin can I was after. So Ted comes out to where I'm at and says, 'Ben, do you vant a little help vith that?' 'Sure, Ted, but I don't know if it can be sighted in at all.' Ted takes the rifle and scrutinizes it carefully, firing off one test shot. 'Hm. Vell, I think I know vat the problem is.' He gets out a smaller pocket knife and makes a few minor adjustments, taps the sight once with the butt of the knife, fires one more test shot. 'Okay, now she should vork.' Ted walks to a tree about seventy-five feet away and sticks a wooden match in the bark. Returns to where I'm standing, takes aim freehand, pulls the trigger. The match bursts into flame."

I'd heard over a hundred of those stories about Ted, and there were probably thousands more. Take the time Dad and a couple of other hunters were returning across Murtle Lake in the boat after a day of hunting on the other side. One of them spotted a flight of Canada geese winging their way south and headed on a course that would take them above the boat.

One hunter called out, "Hey, Ted, why don't you shoot one of those and Ben will fix it up for dinner tonight!"

"Yeah, Ted," they all chimed in.

So he killed the motor and asked for his rifle. Now we're not talking your high–end, custom-built, scope-sighted, semi-automatic; that rifle was probably pressed into service against the Kaiser in WWI. The geese were rapidly closing who-knows-how-high above. Ted took aim from a boat filled with onlookers who had probably gotten into the Scotch on the return trip, and fired. One lone goose vaporized in the skies above.

Ted turned to the astonished hunters and replied, "Darn, I ruined him. Do you vant me to shoot another vun?"

The evening had, by now, progressed into bedtime, so we all said our goodnights. Dad and I walked back down the road to our cabin in the cool night air. For the first time, I took notice of the brilliant sky, the absence of city lights or any other light at all. The stars appeared closer than usual up there, and a dead silence pervaded the air. *This truly is a beautiful place*, I thought and would take great pleasure in the peaceful beauty for many days to come.

Morning broke early as Dad had decided on his own to get me conditioned to the idea that the day starts before the sun is up. We had breakfast, and it was now about five thirty. I walked out onto the porch and looked up the road to the farmhouse where the lanterns were lit. Shortly, we walked up to the farmhouse and joined in the morning gathering for coffee. Jennie had already prepared breakfast for the family, and the day was underway. The Two by now were up, the baby had been fed, and Ted had the day laid out. He was getting ready to feed the horses, bring in more wood for the stove, and then sit down to a family get-together over breakfast.

"Good morning, men," Ted said. "I have some things I need to get to today, but I vant to show Paul around the place this morning, and then you two can try your luck at the creek, maybe go for a svim."

That worked for me, as I was excited to check the place out.

After more conversation, Dad, The Two, and I trudged off with Ted to check out first the shop and tack room. That held a real collection of tools, equipment, horse stuff—I didn't know the names then, and a lot of it looked really strange. He had enough gear crammed in the building to fill a warehouse ten times the size, but he knew where every piece was. I would find out during the course of the summer that most all of it was used in the day-to-day operation of a horse farm and guide service. The shop had a slight musty odor, combined with the smell of leather, horse sweat, machinery oil, and rifle cleaning fluids. Dim lighting prevailed, only that which came in through the open doors; the one bulb lit the room only when the generator ran—and that happened on special occasions only!

On the left side of the shop building stood the woodshed, big enough to hold the winter supply of stove wood and wood for the fireplace. That was about the size of a two- car garage, filled to the ceiling.

Ted turned to me and asked, "Do you know how to chop stove vood?"

I replied, "Oh yes, Dad taught me some time ago; I'm real good at that!"

That was probably the dumbest thing I said during this orientation, and I would pay dearly over the summer for my boasting.

We studied his axes, splitting mall, wedges, and a large hatchet/small axe. Some kind souls had obviously labored for years piling up thirty-inch diameter spruce blocks, white birch, and a few other species outside the woodshed, sort of a wood-block mountain. Like a mountain climber, I would challenge that peak over the course of my stay there and possibly conquer it if I didn't chop my leg off first.

South of the farmhouse in the lower pasture (160 acres) sat a large hay barn. That was a loose hay barn: The hay was brought to the barn on a flat wagon and pulled up a slide by a tractor on the other end of the barn. Someone then swung the hay into the barn, and a trip-device on the bottom of the sling opened, and the hay spilled onto the pile. How did the hay get onto the wagon? Paul would have a very strong back when that summer came to an end.

We headed back to the farmhouse for another large dinner. Those people ate an incredible amount of food, yet no one looked overweight. I'd probably gained five pounds since I'd arrived, and I started to worry about going home looking like Oliver Hardy. I just hoped I'd find enough work to keep me in shape for the summer. (Obviously, some kind of a fog swirled around me. Enough work?) A constant flow of meats, vegetables, potatoes, gravy, and, oh look—another pie—filled the table and our bellies.

After dinner we went into the north pasture (another 160 acres), and I was introduced to the pride of the farm, the horses. When I was about nine years old I'd gone to a riding academy for a couple of weeks of horse lessons. Those horses, trained to walk or canter around an arena, had been pretty docile and never really challenged your commands.

Ted had about two dozen or so, a rather interesting bunch and all very curious about me. It turned out they were having a conversation amongst them.

"Okay, gang, it looks like the old man is going to turn one of us loose to the goofy kid with the short haircut and pink hands. Don't anyone of us cave into him. Bite him whenever possible, and keep him off your back."

This turned out to be a real pact they struck and stuck with, as I was very naive to "real horses."

"Paul, you pick out a horse that you think vould be a good vun to ride for the summer. I vill tell you if it's a good vun."

The first pick was Ted's personal horse, which drew a round of laughter from The Two. I then went through another handful that were described as questionable. I think all of them were missing a few branches at the top of the tree from the rigors of their pack trips, such as carrying a fourteen-foot wooden boat on their back upside down for twenty-five miles. I was told that Minnie one time walked off the trail and slid down the hill upside down with the boat on her back like a bobsled. She arrived at the bottom of the hill unhurt but very wide eyed. After some calming words from Ted and a little gentle coaxing, horse and large boat returned to the trail and proceeded on. Minnie was Dad's favorite riding horse. She was obviously a patient dear and tolerated a great deal.

I finally settled on a good sized chestnut with white socks, Ranger by name. He claimed to be a good sport, showed nice teeth (sharp), and Ted claimed he had a "REAL GENTLE DISPOSITION."

"Ve'll saddle him up and go for a ride tomorrow."

As we walked away, I turned back for a look at the horses. They were all holding their hooves over their faces and guffawing at Ranger, who was scowling and making sarcastic remarks about me. This was going to be a real test of wits. City boys might have street smarts, but they have little training of horses.

At supper, Dad announced that he would stay one more day and leave the following morning. Another evening, this time on the shade porch, as the evenings were starting to heat up. The night air is pleasant on the porch, screened in, as the mosquitoes were also enjoying the evening festivities and looking for an easy meal.

Ted lit his pipe and told us of the time he bought a fine saddle horse from someone in the area. The horse came with an extensive amount of training for riding and hunting. That is to say, it had been conditioned to gunfire so as not to spook and rein-trained so that a hunter could dismount in a hurry, drop the reins, and the horse would not move anymore than a few feet. Ted took the horse on several trips into the park, and the horse behaved well, until one occasion when, upon dismounting, the horse sped off fifteen miles back to the corral. Ted gave him one more chance, and the same thing happened. He returned the horse to the seller, delivering it in the back of his truck after he had shot it so that no other hunter or guide would ever fall prey to the same situation. Lives depended on an obedient horse in areas way off the beaten path.

That was a new side of Ted that I saw the first time. I frequently tell people of the man and his less serious moments, but this other side of him needs mentioning to show that many years of experience had rendered him into a keen hunter, guide woodsman, and survivor.

We retired for the night, and again sleep came to me only much later. I lay in my sleeping bag for what seemed like hours, pouring over what I thought the summer would bring and the fact that Dad would leave in two days. Our relationship had always been good. He had gone out of his way to provide me with companionship, teaching me what he knew, trying to keep me on the right path, and occasionally throwing in bits of humor. Dad had a background like many of his generation—growing up in the Depression, working full-time when he was only thirteen, and struggling to keep his family cared for in the absence of his father. His father died from pneumonia when my dad was a child, and the immediate family helped out as long as they could. As time would prove out, I benefited from his hard-working approach to life and a few other informally introduced lessons. Memories, musings, expectations clouded around me, and sleep overtook my thoughts as another day rose in hot pursuit of me.

Morning arrived sooner each day as I conditioned myself for the inevitable waking to the crow of the rooster. I always wondered why he had to get up so early and make all that noise. All he did was eat, walk around checking everything out, and chase the hens. He wasn't putting up hay, catching horses, fishing, or running a horse ranch.

Dad and I put together a breakfast and enjoyed a bit of conversation over coffee and all the fixings. When we saw Ted and The Two stirring out by the tool-shed, we walked back up the road and joined them. Ted had brought out some horse gear and an empty bucket.

Another First for Everyone

"Ve vill go up in the pasture. I vill show you how to bring the horses down to the fence for picking out the vuns ve vill ride today."

Yee Haw!

Another beautiful day lay before us, and the air filled us with the smells of lush vegetation, evergreens, grass, and the occasional smoke of the wood stove that burned twenty-four hours a day. (Ate a ton of wood, too.) The pastures were getting tall with grass, and mowing had already started in some parts of the farm. After a bit of explanation of the proper names of some of the gear for the horses, we all headed into the north pasture to round up the horses. Dad, Ted, and I each carried a hackamore, a bridle of sorts without the bit. Ted stopped and put a bit of gravel in the bucket.

I politely asked, "What's the gravel for?"

Ted replied, "The horses think ve have brought them a treat of grain. I shake the bucket; they come right avay."

We approached the herd, and sure enough, he shook the bucket, whistled a bit, and we were surrounded with what looked to me like no escape. Ted showed me how to get the halter on Ranger, and handed me the lead. He continued to get his horse and one for Dad.

Now Ranger, being a very observant horse, suddenly realized that he was being held by the funny new kid on the farm. He responded by starting to walk off with me in tow, as though I wasn't even there.

"Whoa. Stop. Stand still. Freeze. Are you listening?"

None of those commands worked.

Ted yelled out, "Vhoa!" and every horse in the herd froze in its tracks, like pause on the DVD player.

Ted turned to me and said, "Don't be afraid to be firm vith the horse till he understands that you are in charge now."

That logic takes awhile to sink in with old Ranger as he had my number and planned on playing it as often as possible. By now, we each had our horse and moved down the field with them in tow, followed by the rest of the gang, figuring they were going out too, so it must be oats for everyone today. We arrived at the gate and somehow got the three horses through without the rest escaping.

After tying up at the hitching rail in front of the house, we started dragging out blankets, bridles, and the saddles. Jennie came out with little Harold and spoke softly to the horses, rubbing their necks and patting them. They enjoyed her attention but not quite as much as the bag of oats they were working on at the moment.

"So you've picked Ranger as your horse for the summer, Paul?"

"Yes, ma'am," I replied. "He seems to like me. I think we're going to get along real well."

That had to be one of the most naïve things I'd ever said in my life. Ranger responded with a shake of his head and passing of a large volume of gas.

Then Ted came over to help me prepare the beast for the day's riding.

"Now pay attention. He is a good horse, but you must be firm vith him. Sometimes he likes to run the show."

Ted started with the bridle; the bit slipped into his mouth in a flash. Ranger's eyes grew big as the blanket was put on his back. Ted then placed the saddle and did up the belly strap. As he doubled up the cinch strap, Ranger's stomach seemed to double in size and a bored look came over his face. Ted chuckled as he placed his knee against the horse's stomach and drove it halfway to his spine. Ranger sucked in wind like a giant bellows, and Ted took up all the slack on the cinch strap.

Another First for Everyone

"Don't be fooled by this big guy," Ted said, "or your saddle vill be underneath him on the trail. And so vill you!"

Future encounters with Ranger made me a wiser young man.

Dad, Ted, and I were now ready for the ride. Almost. We couldn't leave without food, and Jennie had prepared us a "small" lunch. We said good-bye to all. The Two were not happy about being left behind; it didn't make sense to them.

I secured the reins, climbed aboard, and down the road we went. Well, that didn't seem so bad. Ranger behaved nicely and seemed content with all my commands. That is, till we got to a point where the trees were close to the trail. He suddenly developed an itch and, oblivious to the fact that I was supposed to be in charge, veered off the trail, under a low hanging branch, which nearly decapitated me, and leaned into a very large tree, positioning my leg between the tree and his side. No amount of yelling or attempts to rein him in seemed to work till he felt relieved of the itch. Quite pleased with himself, we proceeded down the trail, occasionally trying the low-branch thing and just stopping for the sake of stopping. It would be weeks before Ranger and I came to a negotiated agreement. (Treats!)

Later we returned to the farm and helped put away the horses and tack (saddles, bridles, blankets, all that stuff) and had a light early dinner. Ted suggested that we go out and maybe do a little haying. Dad liked this idea, as he could get some pictures of Ted and me doing what I would, in the weeks to come, discover bordered on forced hard labor. The nearest thing to haying I'd ever done was mowing the lawn. Kind of the same thing, grass and all, collect it, put it in the compost bin. Ted's bin was a wee bit bigger, however, big enough to store hay for two dozen horses for the entire winter.

Ted got out the tractor, complete with a side mower, or sickle mower, which I would become very familiar with as the weeks went by. We did a little cutting, Dad taking pictures, all very fun, and the job seemed like it might be a nice way to get a bit of exercise and sunshine. Ted showed me how the hay is coiled in rows and then forked onto the bed of the wagon, and finally loaded into the hay barn. *OK, I thought, works for me. A couple hours of this every day, no sweat.*

Later that evening after supper, we all sat around the dining table exchanging light conversation. Ellen and Jim listened to my stories about life in the big city—sidewalks, paved streets, stoplights, and ice cream shops. Meanwhile, Dad walked down to our little cabin and came back with something wrapped in a piece of cloth. Of course, we all looked on over generous helpings of pie prepared by Jennie that day.

"What is it?" we all asked.

Dad proceeded to tell a short story. "Some years ago, when I was up here with the boys, we traveled up on South Plateau for moose and deer. The hunting was good, we had good weather, and everyone got along great. Now in the evening, a bit of spirits and cards took up the time, mostly fun, and a little bit of betting. As the evening wore on, the betting got pretty serious, and Ted was falling behind a bit. I proposed he put up something of real value, like his faithful sheath knife.

"Now this is no ordinary knife, handmade by none other then Ted himself from a sawmill blade, ground and polished to a keen edge and a stag-horn handle, carved to fit. This is no cheap factory knife, and I wanted it. I said, 'Ted why not bet the knife?' 'Vot? You vant me to bet my knife?' Ted put up the knife reluctantly, I won the hand—and a piece of Ted Helset.

"So here's the deal, Ted. By summer's end, take Paul to one of your secret fishing spots, and find him the biggest fish. If he catches it, the knife is yours." Dad opened the cloth, and there it was, a true piece of handcraft. Ted's eyes got suddenly big,

Another First for Everyone

and then shrank back to normal size as his mind started plotting where this fish was.

"Ve will find that fish by the end of summer. I vill get the knife back!"

Dad rolled the knife back in the cloth and handed it to me. "Keep this safe; it's not his yet!"

We all laughed, said our goodnights, and headed back to our cabin.

Overhead held unusual clarity that evening, and we sat on the porch for a spell, watching the northern lights curtain across the skies above the park. Dad recalled his trips up north, the time spent away from the hectic pace of home, and the opportunity to escape from life in the city and commune with nature and all her wonders and tranquility.

"Paul, you've come to a place where life moves at a different pace, for a different reason, and the reward is the challenge of survival and adventure. I've always wondered why I took the fork in the road I did and not this one. Maybe it was the hard times my family came up against with the death of my father. Maybe it was my need to be successful. At any rate, take as much as you can away with you this summer. This is your adventure. This is the moment when your heart and soul are ready to grow up and face obstacles on your own. I had a few adventures in my young adult life. They made a difference; that's why I wanted this for you."

This all made a lot of sense. Dad never wavered in his determination about anything. He continually preached a line of be tough, yet now he knew that I needed to bond that philosophy with an adventure using tools he had given me in my life. A few years later, he gave me a poem for my eighteenth birthday, Rudyard Kipling's *If*, which pretty much summarized his view on how a man should carry himself through life. I knew that this summer would bring changes in my life. It would take me to places I had not yet seen and give me experiences I had not yet had. Dad had campaigned hard for this trip. He saw I was at a crossroads, and he hoped I would take the road best suited for me. Only time would tell.

As usual, the morning came early, what with the added activity of getting Dad's stuff packed and cleaning the cabin out. I was moving to the farmhouse. My bed would be a canvas cot on the front porch. The Helset family seemed excited about my coming to live with them for a spell. Jennie found a place for my stuff, The Two found my cot and sleeping bag a great place to jump up and down, and Ted found pleasure in the prospect of another set of hands on the farm—and, I suspected, a chance of getting his knife back.

That breakfast bustled with conversation, intermixed with generous portions of Jennie's home cooking. Their oldest son, Roy, and Marlene and their baby came over for the morning meal and a chance to say good-bye to Dad. Roy was always one of Dad's favorites on the hunting and fishing trips, young but keen in the ways of the woods and never shy about work. Over the summer, I would get to know more about that young man and how much he reflected his dad.

Following breakfast, Dad and I went back to the cabin, loaded his stuff into the Buick, and drove back over to the farmhouse. Dad made a special effort to say good-bye to each and everyone, baby Harold included. He reminisced a bit with Roy, told him to keep me out of mischief, tousled The Two's hair, and gave Jennie a hug. He thanked her for all she had done to make our stay a pleasant one and her special touch with the cooking.

"Ted," he said, "keep this boy busy and teach him a thing or two about farm life and the way of the woods. You have always been a good companion on our trips up here. Thank you for everything."

Another First for Everyone

When it came to good-byes, Dad was never too long winded. That was in contrast to other times, when he had more than enough to say.

He turned to me. "Paul, take care of yourself, write, and help out around here. He shook my hand, gave me the traditional whack on the chest with the back of his hand and a look that told me he was on the verge of breaking down. I would not see that look again, till over thirty years later, when he and I talked, a week before he died.

Dad and the Buick took off down the road, turned beyond the bridge over Hemp Creek and disappeared out of sight. I stood there wondering, first, if he would be okay and, second, what was in store for me next. Without another moment for such reflections, Jim and Ellen each took a hand and started dragging me back to the house. Everyone went back in, and the women headed for the kitchen. Roy had the day available to help Ted, so it was decided that this was as good a time as any to get after the haying for a few hours.

Ted grinned at me. "Come, Ve vill get those hands in shape in no time. Let's put up some hay!"

The real saga had begun.

That Summer

The structure of every aspect of my daily life was about to change dramatically. I really thought—hoped—it would be for the good, as I was about to immerse myself without my own family for support into an existence with, I had been told, a wonderful bunch of people. But I held some reservations. At this time in my life, away from home had consisted of an occasional overnight visit to my grandmother and neighborhood sleepovers—all with people I knew quite well and for stays far less than a whole summer.

The Helset family and others would go to great lengths with compassion, involvement, understanding, and a heck of a lot of patience to make that a good summer. They knew nothing of my background, with the exception of whatever Dad had conveyed to Ted and Jennie. They were people who dealt with situations directly, no philosophy or mind games, and got the job done. Everyone worked hard and enjoyed eating and the time that was available to play or explore. Sleep was something cherished, as there was little of it on an operation like this. The few hours for slumber reminds me of Ben Franklin who, it is said, got only four hours or less every night. The length of time you spent sleeping didn't matter as much as the depth of it. I remember in that summer little about the time between when my head hit the pillow and when I next opened my eyes.

The next few days after Dad left were immediately taken up with the task of getting the hay cut, raked, coiled, and stacked. Concern about the weather always hung over us as rain would stop the whole operation. I came to a real understanding of the expression, "Make hay while the sun shines." A sizeable amount of hay already lay cut and on the ground, so the next step in the process was to rake it into rows. Ever see one of those rake machines on a farm? It has two big steel wheels with spokes and a seat up high with a giant set of rake tines behind it. Whenever I saw one, I always cringed at the idea of riding one and falling off the seat and being skewered. I never dreamed that the day would come when I would be told, "Now climb up there, sit on the seat, and put your feet on the pedals." It sounded easy enough, except when I sat down and looked below and behind me, my feet wouldn't stop shaking long enough to get them on the pedals. Seat belts were not part of the program either, but a nice long handle on the right side gave one a feeling of some stability. Pushing down on one of the pedals raised the rake, and pushing the other pedal lowered it. The long handle was only a guide, but I thought I had to use it each time to raise the rake so that halfway through the day my entire right palm was one giant blister with tinges of red around the edge.

Ted realized my mistake and told me, "Just push the pedal; don't push on the handle. It vill come up by itself."

But he failed to mention if you pushed the other pedal at the wrong time, the rake would thrash wildly like the jaws of a crocodile, as the whole machine shook wildly trying to throw

*Paul and Ted cutting hay
1961*

you into its tines of death! Many hours of raking, sometimes even late after supper, made me appreciate life on the farm.

Once we had raked the hay into long rows, we raked it into loose piles for stacking into field stacks. Francis, the hired hand, and I were put to work trimming the hay stacks, a job that required a little bit of experience. The object was to build the stack right so that two people could pitch it onto the flatbed wagon in one effort. Of course, it required a degree of strength, which I would not develop until I was near the end of haying season. Francis was an acquaintance of Roy's and a very hard worker. He had experience at almost everything, and I paid close attention to learning from him. Ted and Francis would continually coax me into doing a little more than I had, thus strengthening me and allowing me to sleep a lot better.

We would, by rule, stop mid-morning and take a break in the shade of the hay barn in the south pasture. We all spent the time telling really far-fetched hunting and fishing stories and partaking in a most unique treat for me, homemade root beer. Jennie made this in used beer and soda bottles from a Hires root beer base and capped it. It would ferment in the bottles and then be retired to the ice house. During these breaks, she or The Two would deliver it in a burlap sack with the wet sawdust from the icehouse clinging to the cold bottles. The first gulp would hit me like an electric shock, that delicious cold beverage contrasting with the stifling summer heat. What a memory of summer days and hard work.

Getting the hay off the wagon and into the barn required a wee bit of engineering and ingenuity. Ted had constructed a slide at one end of the barn on which the entire wagon load of hay was pulled up by means of a tractor at the other end of the barn. The hay was loaded on a rack of sorts constructed of poles and ropes and connected over the haystack on top. Under

Paul loading the hay wagon
1961

Hay being pulled into the barn
1961

the load was a trip device, a long rope used to dump the load of hay as it swung into the barn. As the hay load swung wildly in the air above, one would watch for the right place and time to trip the load to the proper corner of the barn. After many loads tripped by either Roy or Francis, the authorities decided Paul should take over this chore. I climbed the ladder attached to the inside wall of the barn and hung on with one hand as the load left the ramp. Now back then, I was pushing about 135 pounds, so half a ton of hay swinging overhead had the potential of creating a mild disaster. As the load swung into the spot I had picked, I gave the trip rope a hard jerk and...nothing happened except the load swung away from me, jerking me off the ladder into mid-air and under the hay load. The additional weight of me, hanging on the rope, tripped the load above me. It only took a few minutes to dig me out, once again, to much laughter at my expense. I was becoming the main attraction of comedy hour at Hemp Creek.

On one occasion as we took our break in the shade of the north side of the hay barn, I got my first glimpse of Ted Helset the outdoorsman and adventurer.

Ted, Francis, Roy, and I were enjoying the cold root beer, delivered by none other than The Two, while Roy told stories of adventure in the woods and fish stories with no apparent limits on size and quantity. Ted was sitting next to me and in a flash of his hand removed my sheath knife from its cover on my left side. I blinked in amazement at the ease by which he had performed that trick as he tossed the knife end over end. He seemed amused with it, but I questioned its worth. The knife was the one I had bought at home; I had paid next to nothing for it, and the quality reflected its true monetary value.

"This is a pretty good knife. It needs a little sharpening, and it vill do the job."

Ted's observations were polite, yet I questioned the ability of the knife to do much of anything. I replied, "It's not a real good knife. You couldn't throw it or anything like that." Spoken like a true knife thrower, I couldn't throw a knife through an open barn door.

Ted's blue eyes stared through me, and a challenge was put in place. To our left was a row of fence posts. He first flipped the knife blade into his hand and then picked out a post at least thirty feet away. Standing up, he pitched the knife, and it stuck in the post with a resounding thud. I looked at it for what seemed like eternity.

Ted responded, "Vot do you mean you can't throw it?"

I spent most of the summer hunting down unsuspecting fence posts and knocking them senseless with the handle end of the knife.

The summer haying went on for weeks. Neighbors would occasionally come by and help, and we would reciprocate with the same for them. Pay for helping came as a really hardy meal and much thanks to those who had participated. Between the haying and the continuous eating, I started to put on a little weight and none of it flab. Ranger noticed the change, too, and began questioning whether he could keep up his charade. With my growing strength, I became more confident and less intimidated by his size. He, in turn, began to warm up to the attention I offered him in the form of contact, gentle nudges, and sometimes more physical direction.

Haying was hot and tiring, but the afternoon break always had time for a dip in some cool, refreshing waters. Following the noon meal ("dinner" in farm parlance), The Two and I would don swim wear and head for a well-deserved reprieve. But as I learned early on, they couldn't swim! There was a good size pool in the north pasture, which I turned into the training center for these pint-size students. Jim was excited about the promise of learning to swim as his dad would not allow him to travel to Stillwater till he had learned. (I found out years later that Ted could not swim either, but he was the boss!) By the end of the summer, Jim was swimming with ease, challenging anything that Hemp Creek could throw at him with determination and bravado. Ellen was content to splash and paddle about, throwing water at me and making sure she got equal amounts of attention. Jim's hard work would pay off in the weeks to come; we would all travel to Stillwater.

Activity was the mainstay of life on the Helset farm. Not a minute was wasted watching TV or sitting with nothing to do. I, for one, took up whittling with one of my "sharp" knives and proceeded to carve all sorts of wood pieces up into unique objects of The Two's liking, one of them being wooden swords. These were made from wooden cedar shakes, had a nice cross handle, and were useful for slaying evildoers, dragons, or an occasional grizzly bear and, of course, for hand-to-hand combat, of which I was always the villain.

Shortly after Dad left, I returned to the aforementioned woodshed and sized up the supply of stove wood. The pile was down to probably a couple of days' worth, what Ted had been able to cut for Jennie between other duties on the farm. I confronted Ted about the idea of my working on that a few hours in the evenings to fill in the time.

"That vould be very good. In fact, I have a proposal for you. Split the vinter's supply for Jennie. I vill pay you twenty-five dollars!"

That was joy to my ears. Twenty-five dollars clinched the deal. I could put that kind of money to work when I got home—the first down payment on a car when I turned sixteen, fireworks for the next Fourth of July, school supplies when I...no forget that one.

The next evening I got started, laid out my game plan, sharpened the tools, and got to work. My first attempts to bust the giant blocks of spruce were painful and labor intensive. As time went on, I developed systems of mass production and motion-saving steps. The Two found amusement in my attempts to streamline the process but soon grew bored with watching. However, I pressed them into service stacking and keeping the area policed up. The pile of blocks and rounds was enormous, such that I saw myself staying on into the winter just to get that season's supply done before I left. Every evening available that didn't involve haying or some other activity, I spent in the woodshed, working towards that twenty-five dollars. My hands will never forget the work they did that summer; I still, today, go back to those evenings anytime I pick up an axe or splitting maul.

At some time wandering around the farm, closer to the mountain, Jim had brought my attention to the rabbit population along the borders of the hay fields. "Those are rabbits Mom and Dad let go, and we shoot them once in a while for dinner."

Hey, that sounded like fun. All we needed was the rifle, which Jennie supplied with a box of 22 cartridges, and off we went in pursuit of tomorrow night's dinner. I had no idea how many critters constituted a rabbit dinner, but I did not want to short the meal. I think we dispatched seven or eight before the smoke cleared. She had only wanted two or three. Life with Paul on the farm posed its challenges for them as much as adapting to a new way of living provided me with "opportunities for growth." They got through it, for sure, but a learning process was in store for all of us as I tended to do most things in excess, wanting to please and earn the respect of people who were not sure yet that I could fill the request.

.

Those Giant Rainbow Trout

Now just what determines that a trout be considered a giant? It's completely in the hands—or mind—of the fisherman describing the encounter. I describe, hereafter, various encounters between fish and Paul as truthfully and accurately as any experienced fisherman would of events that took place forty years ago. The trout ranged in size from eight inches to much more than that and,… Well,…let the story tell the rest. Giant rainbows were, of course, at the top of the scale, and the pursuit was always to try and connect with the giant.

Hemp Creek, up to this point, was my official fishing hole and often shared with The Two. We would trek across the field or go down to the bridge and rustle up trout for dinner or breakfast the next day. In later years, I would reflect on these expeditions as times that probably amused Ted to no end because the kids and I entertained ourselves with trout the size of a hot dog. Those trout were fun, though, biting on my homemade flies, periwinkles, caddis fly larvae, and just about anything else. Jim always maintained a lead over me with natural bait versus my flies, but I was determined to put my handiwork to use. Only in weeks to come would I graduate into the big leagues of trout fishing.

On one occasion, Jim and I challenged each other to a bait-versus-fly contest of sorts. At some point we lost our minds or, more accurately, the number of fish we had stashed as we worked our way down the creek. Once again, I had overdone in my attempt for respect and recognition. Jim and I were in possession of a limit probably fifty or seventy-five over the amount allowed by law. After a short sermon by Ted and Jennie, we were set to the task of cleaning all those beautiful trout. That afternoon, Roy drove us to a survey camp outside the park, where we presented trout dinner to the camp cook, who thanked us endlessly for our efforts. Several dozen members of the camp enjoyed a trout dinner that evening, and they probably still talk about the two boys who walked into their camp that day with a whole lot of almost giant trout.

Okay, this is the beginning of the fishing stories that still bring the hair up on the back of my neck. By this time in my life, trout were measured as legal if they were longer than the distance across your hand, from the tip of your baby finger to the tip of your thumb. I could count on my two hands trout I had caught bigger than that, excluding the ones from Canyon Creek Trout Farm, north of Seattle. I was about to be baptized, washed, immersed, and near drowned into big boys' fishing.

Roy and his family showed up for dinner one evening, and the conversation at one point turned to the subject of fishing on the North Thompson River below the farm. Ted and Roy were discussing Dolly Vardens (also known as bull trout in the States) that were moving up the river and schooling in the still waters and eddies. My ears, of course, by now had grown twice their original size and were perpendicular to the side of my head, or possibly slanted a wee bit forward.

Ted spoke. "Maybe you should take Jim and Paul to the big log jam and try your luck. Those brutes are really big this year, people say."

A small thud was heard, as Jim fell out of his chair. I never figured out if he fainted or lost his balance.

Roy replied, "I have a day off after tomorrow. Could you boys be ready at five thirty in the morning? Don't want to miss the bite, which falls off by noon or sooner."

We both nodded, dumbfounded, as if lightning had just erupted through the front door. Ellen expressed her total dissatisfaction at the idea, which did not include her, so Jennie came up with some ideas on how they would spend that day.

The next day was taken up with mindless work, or so it seemed at the time. I could not concentrate on anything but being pulled into the raging river by fish longer than the distance across my hand. Jim was no help, attached to me like a leech, planning our next day's conquest of these vast herds of **Giant Dolly Varden!** We carefully laid out our fishing gear, my big knife for cutting myself loose from one of these brutes that were going to drag me down the river, and various lures. That evening, wood cutting seemed hard to concentrate on. We sat on my cot on the front porch and talked late about tomorrow.

Daylight came late that morning, but I was awake before it showed its face coming from across the creek. Ted and Jennie were already up, and breakfast and coffee were headed for the table. Jim and I nodded at each other as we entered the dining room, acknowledging each other's presence at the morning meeting of the Hemp Creek Fishing Club.

Roy showed up shortly, and greetings were exchanged all around. Jennie served up a hearty breakfast, and the conversation ensued.

"So how big do you think those Dollies are, Roy?" Ted asked.

"Well, big but not as big as the trout at Stillwater the last few years and not quite as feisty."

Okay, they cast the bait, I took it, and they reeled me in, nice and slow.

"Not as big as the trout at Stillwater? What size are we talking about?"

Ted replied between bites, "The Dollies coming up the river range, usually, four to six pounds, sometimes bigger. Ve don't keep a scale at Stillvater, but we've seen trout that probably vould go ten-plus pounds. But then there was that one fish two years ago that ve never got to the boat."

Roy cut in, following a swig of coffee I thought would drown him, "I remember it ran for the boat, swam right under us. I saw its head on one side, jumped to the other side, and there was its tail!"

Ted put his coffee down. "It spooled the fisherman's reel, probably seventy-five, a hundred yards of line, just kept going down river."

Both men resumed eating. Jim and I stopped with forks mid-air above the plate, and mouths wide open.

Jennie appeared and broke the trance. "I have lunches packed for you. Roy if you catch enough fish, maybe stop at some of the folks on the way back and see if they want to trade anything for the evening meal."

"See if my family wants to come over for supper," Roy replied, "and maybe Clara and Ralph."

I was suspicious of that exchange. How would we all eat on a couple of pan-sized Dollies. I knew there was no such thing as four-to-six pound Dollies. This was going to be an interesting day.

Shortly, Roy, Jim, and I were in the old Chev pickup, headed back down the road towards Clearwater, maybe four to five miles. We turned off the road at the Fosse place, parked, and headed off on a trail to the canyon where Fight Creek lies. It was another four or five miles to the river and a treacherous hike down into the canyon. Upon arriving, I was astounded by the enormous log jam in the river. Years of high water had produced a pile of logs and stumps as big as a house, wedged in between large rocks and rock walls, holding the mass of timber captive.

We followed Roy across the log jam to a place where some open water showed between the logs and a rock outcropping. He pointed into the water, and they were there, gently moving in the slow water with their bright red spots showing, as big as artillery shells and almost as powerful, I was to soon find out, the fish that would feed the legions back at the farm, **GIANT DOLLY VARDEN…**

"So, how are we going to land these brutes, Roy?" I inquired.

"We'll hook them. I'll climb out on that big log, and you guys lead them over to me."

That seemed simple enough—tie on a spoon and just lead them to Roy. I went first, using a bamboo pole with a small open faced reel, and tossed in the spoon. About five seconds elapsed. Those fish had probably never seen a spoon, much less one on a string. The impact was like hooking a '62 Chrysler. The fish took an immediate plunge to the bottom of the pool, catching me off-guard, and the pole snapped like a wishbone. Now I had a total mess, a crazed fish, two sticks with line attached, and Roy calling, "Lead him over this way!" The fish finally pulled hard enough he broke the line at the spoon.

Roy was probably not amused at the depth of the amateur display I had put on, trying to get control of that fish, but he didn't show it. Immediately he came up with a better idea.

"Let's try something else. There's another way to capture these big guys."

The log jam, in its birth, had pushed up against the rocks, thus creating a sort of cavern underneath. Roy had discovered this on previous adventures and was about to reveal it to us. We all clamored down off the topside and stood on the rocky beach, each removing shoes, socks, and trousers. We then carefully wove our way inside the log cathedral to the cramped inner chamber. Light filtered down into the water from above, thus creating a sort of aquarium appearance. My jaw once again unhinged as I gazed into the clear water at dozens of fish lazily resting in the shallows of the pool.

"Now what, Roy?" I asked as he started moving into the cool water.

"Be very quiet, and just watch."

He moved out into an area where the fish were schooled up and gently slid his hand down over a large fish. The fish moved forward up current, and then slowly slid back to where it had been resting. Roy's hand, however, had not moved. He had his thumb and fingers spread wide apart, and the fish slid right into his grasp. He clamped down on its gills, and up it came. As it cleared the surface of the water, the tight space we occupied exploded with water, and the silence was broken with shouts of success.

Each of us attempted Roy's technique, with mixed success. My first fish just lay there, not at all amused at my grip. As I hoisted him out of the water, he nearly sprained my wrist and fell back into the pool. Jim had no better luck than I, his smaller size being a challenge with the big fish and the water a little deep. Among us, nearly a dozen of the brutes were eventually brought to the shore, and we celebrated with sandwiches and the balance of our lunch.

Roy's attention to us, his patience with such novices, and his extensive experience in the natural world would continue to play in his time with me, both in this fishing expedition and in other adventures that summer. I forever hold those memories close to my heart. Roy had grown up early in life, taking on numerous responsibilities and always looking for an adventure. Bridging the gap between youth and adult, he was a revered older brother to me and as much a mentor as Ted or my father.

Following lunch, we cleaned fish—my first experience with ones as big as your leg. My now famous throwing knife had been baptized into the art of cleaning world-class Dollies. I was quite proud of it, as it was of me, I'm sure. Roy had brought burlap sacks, and we packed them, putting grass around the fish to keep them fresh. Then we climbed out of the canyon, loaded down with close to fifty pounds of fish. The afternoon air was heavier, and the hike out was hot and seemed longer than the hike in, but we labored on, filled with pride in the success of the trip. The sight of the truck brought relief to my aching arms and legs.

On our return trip, we stopped at a few neighbors' farms and handed out dinner. At the Archibald place, Dave and his wife, Gladys, greeted us at the porch, and the gabbing picked up speed. Dave was another outdoorsman and had, on numerous occasions, helped Ted with his haying and guide work. Dad had referred to him in stories and always enjoyed his company. Gladys kept an abundant garden and offered to trade vegetables and raspberries in exchange for fish. Our evening supper continued to take shape as we headed back up to Hemp Creek.

Once back at the Helsets, we were met there, too, at the porch for an examination of our catch of the day. Ellen, having recovered from being left behind, was once again her joyful self. Jenny sorted through our load and proclaimed that supper would be a real feed. Roy, Marlene, and the baby would share dinner with us that night, as would Clara and Ralph and their two, Susan and Mike. Dinner was baked fish, potatoes, vegetables, gallons of fresh milk, and dessert of raspberries and whipped cream.

That particular meal stays fond in my memory because it represents the stuff that families are made of. Work was usually the focus of life on the farm at Hemp Creek—long days in the field, building or fixing something, collecting the essentials of survival, dealing with the occasional emergency. But that focus, however time-consuming, supported the true essence of the family—the time together, the love for each other, and the sharing of one's self. That was a lifestyle I had not had much exposure to, if any, to be honest, and for that reason it remained close to my heart.

What Crisis?

Life at Hemp Creek always seemed to hover a notch above exciting. Sometimes events involved pain; sometimes they gave a thrill unlike any I'd had until then; sometimes they provided experiences I would never again have the opportunity to witness in my relatively sheltered urban life. I never knew what new adventure awaited me, but I did know that one lurked just around the corner, nearly every single day.

Fencing was an important ingredient of the farm, and it required continuous upgrading and repair. Animals actually love fences and the mental exercise they provide; they occupy their extensive leisure time behind them devising ways to get on the other side. Having accomplished that feat, they turn the game over to the humans to take responsible action and make improvements and (try to) outsmart them.

Not having a lot of experience in this department, I gave Ted fresh meat to work with. I learned that there are smart ways to address barbed wire and some ways too painful to mention. Rolling out, tensioning, stapling, setting posts, all factored in a day's work on fences. By the time I attacked the fences (or was it the other way around?), I had become familiar with the gray Ford tractor. It was a lumbering beast with all the usual farming capabilities plus the ability to perform numerous other chores. Ted would entrust me, on some occasions, to drive while he managed another aspect of the chore.

On one of those occasions, he had me drive as we tensioned up a stretch of new fence. I eased the tractor ever so slowly as the wires tightened, and I got the order to hold it there. I missed the clutch, and the wire gave way, screaming through the air. I escaped with minor scratches and cuts. Ted, of course, being the experienced one, had positioned himself out of harm's way. The crises had been a minor one, although one filled with memorable lessons for me.

Barbed wire, another time, proved to be much more painful for one of the horses. This particular horse had probably been spooked by wildlife in the lower pasture near the creek. Ted had noticed her missing that morning, and we set out on a search. In breaking through the fence, she had tangled her hoof in the wire and cut it badly. Ted calmed the animal down while I ran to the tack shed for a halter and wire cutters. Upon my return, Ted secured the halter, and I held the lead. He talked endlessly to the horse as we walked along, assuring her that he was trying to help. His words—or the feeling behind them—worked magic on the animals. There was a mystique between him and the horses; they always communicated on a higher plane. Having cut the horse free, we led her back to the house and shed. Jenny came out with an assortment of bandages and preparations, and they commenced doctoring while The Two and I watched quietly and felt the horse's grief. I wasn't confident the horse would survive all that injury, but she was in excellent hands that knew the limits of injury. By the end of summer, she was fully healed and once again ready for adventure.

What Crisis?

Injury would take its toll on another horse that summer, and once again, that tireless pair would be there in attendance. This time a horse had gotten into the heavy brush after fleeing the bonds of confinement and had harpooned himself on a dead branch, piercing his chest to the ribcage. Ted assessed the damage and proceeded to clean the wound while I soothed the horse. Jennie prepared a gauze dressing with ointment, and they tucked it into the wound for several days or more.

These accidents were a disruption but not uncommon on a farm or ranch. The workings of the place—and everyone else in it—depended upon all people and animals functioning at full health at all times. Accidents happened; those in charge took action to ensure the livelihood of all. The formula was simple, but the execution of it sometimes strained even the most accomplished.

The single worst accident occurred years back when Roy was just a boy and Clara just entering her teens. One fall in the late forties, Ted had contracted to guide several hunters on a hunting expedition in the park. After several days, Ted had an idea to put the hunters in a stand, and he would circle around a small mountain and drive game ahead of him. While moving through the woods, he attempted to cross over a large slippery log and fell. His left leg snapped above the knee, and he went into momentary shock. Moments went by, and then he quickly started taking inventory of his situation. He still had five miles to cover before he would meet up with the hunting party, and it was growing late in the day. To compound the situation, snow had started falling. His inventory of personal possessions consisted of his rifle, ammo, an orange, matches, and the knife he wore religiously.

Building a fire at that point would only keep him warm—and for only so long. He was too deep in the woods for anyone to see it, and he needed to utilize what strength he had now to maximize his chance for being discovered. He knew he had to get closer to the party before dark. Crawling a ways, he found a sapling and with the knife fashioned it into a usable crutch. He cut two other sticks, removed both his boot laces, and tied the sticks on both sides of the leg to splint it.

Those activities, of course, used up precious time, but he still had his strength and was not ready yet to call it quits. Ted was made of stuff most men only dream about, rarely are exposed to, and seldom in their lives have to apply. The next few days would use up all the strength and will power Ted had in his body and spirit, and he would be forced to consider the one last option—whether to give in if at all.

Ted raised himself from the forest floor, and with the crutch under his left arm and the rifle as a makeshift crutch on the right, he pressed on into the darkness. He was moving on pure adrenalin at that point, but as snow continued to fall he could feel the cold closing in and knew he must keep moving. Between moments of rest and passing out from pain, he remembered seeing lights flashing from atop the mountain, searchers trying to signal him.

At one point that first night, he fell down a hillside in the dark and lost one of his laceless boots. He used up two precious hours and priceless energy retrieving it and crawling back up. At that point, his exhausted, tortured body could take no more, and he blacked out. He did not regain consciousness till daylight the next morning.

He was still in the deep forest, and by his reckoning, he had two miles to go to an old growth burn, where someone might see a signal fire. Knowing that by this time a number of friends and fellow hunters must be out looking for him, he felt the need not to let them down. He must continue on and make it to the burn area. But he covered only a mile that day before darkness stopped him. The pain that second night grew ever

*View of Wells Grey Provincial Park.
2006*

more present and continuously interrupted what little sleep he could snatch. Once again, he considered his options and vowed to make it to the burn the next day.

During this entire ordeal, one thought stayed in the forefront: Jennie and their two children. They meant the world to him, and the thought of returning to them carried him on. Having someone—someones—to live for and falling back on his almost innate survival skills drew him ever closer to rescue and a reunion with his family.

But the following morning found him in worsening condition and losing strength. He covered the final mile to the burned clearing by mid-morning, rested briefly, and began building a series of signal fires. He no longer had the strength or will to continue in any direction. Staying put in the open area with signals burning was his best bet for being found, so he made his stand. Keeping his fires going as best as possible, he reflected in the long hours of waiting on the life he had lived till then—making the long journey from his childhood home in Norway, working his way across Canada, meeting his lovely Jennie, spending their years together in the upper Clearwater valley, raising their two lovely children. All that and prayer kept him going, but the pain and suffering took their toll. His only option, he decided, if he were not discovered by the next day would be to take his own life

In the afternoon it started snowing again, and the Lord intervened. Ted fell into unconsciousness.

Meanwhile, many friends, neighbors, and officials had coordinated for three days, and their efforts paid off. At dusk, a rescue party found the still unconscious body, transported Ted to the nearest road, and rushed him off to the hospital in Kamloops where he remained for six months. He spent nearly two years recovering before venturing into the woods once more.

What Crisis?

That was Ted's greatest test of will and endurance. So many things drove him during those three and a half days. Many men would have succumbed to the pain and fright the first night. Obviously, had it not been for Ted's determination, there would have been no Jim, Ellen, or Harold; no Hemp Creek summer; no opportunity for me to stand in the shadow of that man of so many virtues, to test my abilities and give him the chance to get that much prized knife back. When I asked him about surviving that ordeal, he was very pointed about not giving up when you have the chance. Rudyard Kipling wrote a line in his poem, *If*: "And so hold on when there is nothing in you/Except the will which says to them 'Hold on.'" I have always reflected on that story of Ted's three days, and wondered if I would have made it myself.

Instead of one overwhelming ordeal, I just had an abundance of many mini-adventures, such as the time I fell out of the hayloft and impaled my arm on a rusty nail sticking out of a board. I was sure lockjaw was going to set in.

But Jennie informed me, "Working around the animals, especially the cows, helps to give you immunity." (And I'd thought they were good only for milk!) She inserted the glass iodine swab into the hole in my arm, and the resulting pain chased away any possibility of infection and a moment of my consciousness.

Ranger was behind another attempt to shorten my life, or my stay at Hemp Creek.

It had become my job over the weeks to bring the horses down from the north pasture for pack trips or whatever. I had become familiar and confident with the routine and needed only a halter and bucket with a wee bit of road gravel to pull the job off. Feeling quite sure of myself this time, I walked up the pasture and found the horses. Shaking the gravel bucket,

I soon had the whole herd of nearly two dozen horses trying to get their heads in the bucket at the same time. I moved about, found Ranger, and got the halter on him. Now I had the option of just walking him back down to the fence and picking out the horses for the day or jumping up on him and riding back down bareback! Finding a large rock for mounting, I opted for the ride home. Wouldn't I look snappy coming down the pasture like John Wayne! As we headed out, the herd took the lead. Ranger, being the mount of choice, refused to follow, so he charged toward the front. My heels had a death grip on his ribcage; however, I sensed that I was sliding off the left side. No amount of pulling up on him did any good, and I proceeded to slip further over the side, hanging onto his mane and the rope. By the time we approached the fence next to the road, I had completely slid around, holding onto his neck and hanging under his head with my legs also wrapped around his neck. Ranger finally realized the dilemma I was in and hit the brakes, and I fell to the ground as he gently put one hoof on my chest. He considered crushing me, and then compassion took hold. He put his face close to mine and let out a lengthy snort. Once more, humiliation descended upon me, and I became the star of yet another animal antic for the benefit of the entire Helset family.

That was the last time Ranger went against me. It was as though I had earned the right to call him my horse. We would have many splendid rides in the weeks to come, and he would show me the beauty in the country around the farm and north into the wilderness.

First Pack Trip

Farm life was such an adventure. I had learned so much in the several weeks with the Helsets, honed skills I would never again in my life utilize; appreciated fresh air, good food, deep sleep, and the constant anticipation of what would happen tomorrow. Ted had been patient, as I tested that resource which he regarded as valuable. He seemed pleased with my interest in all he had me do, and I did not shy away from responsibility but welcomed the challenge of more adventure.

By mid-afternoon into my fourth week, we had been loading hay into the hayshed and had reached the end of that cutting. It would be another week before we would cut more, so a break appeared imminent. When the gear had been put away, Ted, Francis, and I sat down to discuss what was next.

"I need to get up to Stillvater to do some repairs on the cabin and make sure things are ready for later in the season. You and Francis vill come with me. Ve vill take three packhorses with some supplies and gear. I think ve vill leave day after tomorrow, so tomorrow is a get-ready day. Paul and I vill go to Clearvater to pick up a few things, and in the afternoon ve vill get all the gear together."

I had waited for those words since I'd seen Ted come riding in with the fishing party when Dad and I had first arrived. This was the stuff real adventures are made of. It was twenty miles or so to Stillwater. Ted had a camp there, one of many in the park. This would be a working trip, but all work and no play make Jack a dull boy, right? This was the place where fish stories originated, from which men returned with broken tackle and looks of despair in their eyes. You didn't go here to fish for dinner; you went to do battle with **GIANT TROUT!**

That night as with many, I stayed up on the front porch and watched the northern lights play in the sky over Stillwater, Murtle Lake, and many other distant places and thought of what lay before me. I'd seen the pictures in Dad's album of the camp at Stillwater and heard the stories of wild game and the encounters too many to tell. One that happened several years after my summer, however, does bear repeating. It was every adventurer's adventure.

Ted and two fishermen from California were up at Stillwater for a week of premium fishing. Both men had been previous guests of the Helsets and were well familiar with the area. One morning Ted went down to the boat to get things ready while the men stayed back at the cabin to get their gear together and pack lunch. Some time passed. Ted waited patiently for the men to come down to the boat, but nothing happened. Ted's patience ran out, and he headed back up the trail to see what the holdup was. As he approached the cabin, he was taken aback by the sight of a large grizzly bear clawing at the front door of the cabin. Obviously the two fishermen trapped inside were beside themselves with fear at their plight.

Ted, being well versed in crises of all kinds and not pleased with a bear making shavings out of his front door, hollered at the bear. The bear was not amused, immediately lumbered off the front porch, and proceeded to approach Ted in a challenging

First Pack Trip

manner, that is to say, sort of side-stepping towards him. At the point where the bear was nearly alongside, Ted unsheathed his hunting knife and drove it into the bear's shoulder area. The bear screamed and lumbered off into the woods, not to be seen again. Ted launched a brief hunt for the wounded bear but at last gave up. He freed the bear's two captive fishermen, and much conversation took place for days afterward.

Now move ahead to that fall, hunting season. Ted had a hunting party at Stillwater and another guide working with him. One day, the other guide and his party, in returning to camp, passed through a nearby cedar swamp and came upon a dead grizzly.

That evening, after dinner, the guide proclaimed, "Ted, I think this belongs to you!" and handed him the knife he had extracted from the dead grizzly's shoulder.

Years later, Ted presented the knife to one of the fishermen who had been held captive by the bear.

Sleep came late for me that night with my mind occupied with thoughts about preparations the next day and an added bonus, a trip to Clearwater. They had bubble gum there, along with whatever Ted needed in the way of serious supplies. As usual, we would also get fifty gallons of gas for the equipment and the truck and tractor. I would get something for The Two; they'd been really good the last week.

The next day, we grabbed breakfast, loaded an empty drum in the truck, and headed south. The twenty-five miles to town seemed to take forever. Upon our arrival, we checked in at the railway station office for a couple of things that had arrived and then tackled the general store and hardware store. We picked up the items for the trip to Stillwater—nails, a few boards, some hardware—then got groceries and gas. I bought a couple of treats for myself and The Two.

A brimmed hat caught my eye, but I wasn't brave enough. That would take another forty years. We visited with a couple of people in the town, stopped in at the post office for the pile of mail, which always accumulated between trips into town, then headed home.

Meanwhile, Francis had been working the morning, organizing some of our stuff for the trip. Ted and I unloaded, had supper, and then we all got to work packing. The Two were not at all happy about being left behind; they would stay home and help Mom with the chores.

Pack boxes were something new to me. They go on the pack frame on each side of the horse and, with other gear, are laced onto the pack frame with a series of fancy knots. Diamond hitches secure the entire load together. It is a very serious and painstaking process loading a packhorse the right way. Extra time taken loading and tying makes the trip more comfortable for the horse and saves time not having to stop every few miles to reload and retie the whole mess.

During the day, Ted carefully explained what we were doing, why we were doing it, and how we should not do it. He had a patience all his own, brought on by years of dealing with clients who came for the adventure, not the details of how to get there or why things must be done the way they are. Sometimes, the client didn't even deal with the preparation end. They'd be flown into Murtle Lake and well cared for by Ted and his crew from that point forward.

I hope by summer's end, perhaps, to get to help with a guided trip on Murtle Lake, I mused. *Probably depends on how things go on this first pack trip.*

All that could be put together the evening before, we did. Then I packed my own things before supper—not a lot, just the bare essentials. I threw in the harmonica and, of course, fishing tackle and only a change of clothes in the event I wound up

First Pack Trip

in the water for some strange reason. I helped Ted with a few last minute details and worked on the growing split-woodpile (still dwarfed by the unsplit portion, but I could see progress in my efforts). My hands had, by now, taken on a huge change from the new lifestyle. Calluses and numerous small cuts and scratches covered the palms of my hands; I saw definition in my arms and felt an overall strength in every part of me.

Supper was the usual blend of good food and conversation. Ted and Francis engaged me in adventuresome conversation about keeping an eye out on the trail for grizzly bears that attack packhorses and cats that pull unknowing riders off their horses and drag them into the darkest part of the woods. This line of dinner table discussion put The Two in that wide-eyed mood and made me the focus of a lot of scrutiny. How much of what the men were telling me was true? The Two counted on me for an honest interpretation later, as to whether they should believe all those wild stories. I chose my words carefully, saying that I had not had the experience yet but would get back to them later.

Ted reached into his shirt pocket. "Paul, these vere at the post office for you today," he said and handed me letters from my mother and dad.

I was momentarily stunned as I looked at the handwriting on the envelopes. It immediately took me home, to the sights, sounds, and smells so familiar to my life, and gave me the sensation of the distance that separated me. Jim wanted me to read them to everyone, but Jennie, bless her heart, reminded him that "These are Paul's, and he will read them later." My heart raced with anticipation of news from home, yet the thoughts of tomorrow held on tight.

That evening, it was warm, and sleeping on the screened porch seemed like a good idea. I sat on the cot and proceeded opening the letters. Mom exclaimed how quiet it was at home and the dog, Duchess, and Sambo, my cat, were aware of my absence. News in the neighborhood was the usual. My friends asked how I was doing and when I'd be home. An underlying tone in Mom's writing let me know she missed me yet understood that I need the experience to grow in self-esteem and spirit. Mom's and my relationship was on and off at that time due to her excessive drinking. Tragically, I was the only male in her life, yet she had to sacrifice me if I were to become the man she so wished me to be. I truly loved her yet grieved for the tragedy her life had become. I knew she was proud, though, that she had raised a son so longing for adventure and a life-changing experience.

Dad's letter, as most men's style of writing to their sons, contained lots of factual information and little emotion. There was however, an underlying message that he was a little envious of my situation and wished there had been more adventures than hard work in his youth. He did have adventures in his adult life, similar to what I was experiencing, but he realized that I needed them as a youth to shape my coming manhood.

The daylight was fading, and I quickly finished my letters. That night in bed, I reflected on all phases of my life to that point. I sensed that things would not be the same when I returned home, nor would they be as simple as before. I knew I needed to think about my future, to decide what I wanted out of life, and to make changes to bring them about. But where to start? What was my calling as a career? Would I someday have a meaningful relationship with a woman, marry, have children? Would I have an impact on their lives, touch them deeply and positively? At this time, I had not chosen any direction in my life, nor contemplated it. I was doing nothing about preparing myself for the next step, distracted by what was going on about me and not encouraged to take up anything that might benefit me as I grew older.

I would draw from this adventure but not fully understand its significance till I was much older and some of the memories had faded. I took a deep breath and smelled the sweet air of cut grass, fir and alder trees, horses and leather. Sleep came fast but not fast enough to keep me from thinking about the morrow and somewhere down the trail where my next adventure waited.

The next morning, neither the daylight woke me nor the rooster but the end of my cot being lifted off the porch floor.

"Let's get going!" a very much awake Ted exclaimed as though he never even went to bed. "Jennie has breakfast vaiting for you. I'll get the gear pulled together. Go round up the horses when you're finished."

I deducted from this hasty awakening that he wanted to get on the trail, the place I would come to understand where he was the most at home. I entered the kitchen to the familiar sounds and smells of breakfast. The Two were not yet up; something must have passed over the house the previous night, taking out everyone under the age of fifteen. Jennie helped me get my meal, which I consumed at supersonic speed. The burns from the hot coffee thrown down my throat would probably heal. No time to worry. I needed to get those horses to the hitching rail!

Something was afoot in the pasture. Miraculously, the horses stood just inside the pasture fence across the road as though a spirit had come to them and announced, "Some of you get to go on a pack trip. First ones to the gate are it!" They waited patiently to be chosen. Of course, some were predestined to go whether they wanted to or not—Ted's black horse, Francis' particular pick, two packers, and of course, good old Ranger.

I carefully sorted them out and led them to the hitching rail at the front of the house, and we applied the assortment of tack to each horse. Most critical to the trip was the placing of the pack frames, their cargo, and the knots used to secure the loads. This time, they mostly carried material for the cabins and their furnishings.

With the last of the gear stored, we tended to our own saddles, bags, and personal effects. I had learned much about saddling Ranger by that time. He even helped a little bit since it was to his benefit, too, if it fit right! By then the old heart started to pump, and I was filled with excitement about yet another new experience—going camping on a horse!

"Got your knife?" Ted inquired.

I pointed to my belt and patted it with a new sense of pride since it had been thrown by Ted and proclaimed to be "not a bad knife at all."

Last item to be loaded aboard was Ted's rifle, a bolt action 30-06 caliber. That rifle was well worn but had not a spec of rust or sign of abuse. It had many an adventure to tell and certainly reflected the pride and experience of its owner. I just sat and watched as he gently slid it into the scabbard in front of the saddle. We were ready, but I was already worn out from the anticipation.

The Two, Jennie, and little Harold all stood by. Ted gave each of the kids a hug, a kiss to Jennie, and a stern nod at me to get mounted, and we were off. Ted took the lead, followed by the two pack animals, then me, and Francis in the rear. To this day, I fondly remember the sound of multiple hooves clopping on the hard gravel road and the sight of the aspen and fir growing nearby and the low-growing grass and plants, dusty from weeks without rain. I had no watch but would have guessed it was about seven o'clock in the morning. Light filtered through the trees on the right side of the road; we were

First Pack Trip

traveling north to the entrance of the park. That endorphin rush you get when your emotions are at their highest filled my heart as I realized I was entering into a new phase of my life, communicating with nature and all of the mysteries it would present about itself.

We continued up the gravel road for about two miles and entered Wells Gray Provincial Park. Clara and Ralph lived at the park entrance and managed the biological aspects and game management within the park boundaries. As we approached their home, Calypso ("Lippy"), the orphan moose, gamboled back to the security of the house and stared at us. The two had taken her in as a small calf and bottle fed her till she was old enough to fend for herself. I was told that, on occasion, she would run in the front door and stand in the security of the living room if she felt challenged by a passing motorist. Our party, evidently, didn't pose such an extreme threat. As we passed by, we waved to them and shortly thereafter left the road and moved into the woods.

The coolness of the morning had started to disappear till we traveled back under cover of the forest canopy. Mosquitoes were now starting to wake up and buzzed lazily around us but, as yet, posed no major assault. Ranger was in his environment now and took to the trail with skill and knowledge of where we were headed. The packhorses hung loose from their leads and maintained a level tempo with Ted in front. Francis smiled in the rear as he observed my head continually spinning in all directions, looking for whatever caught my eye—an errant grouse, squirrel, or chipmunk. The latter would scold us as we passed, and the plant life changed as we went through different levels of light and dark. In one particular area, we ventured into stands of old growth forest that had survived hundreds of years of fire and weather and remained undiscovered by logging. It was a shrine of quiet and tranquility, interrupted only

Calypso the pet moose at Ralph and Clara's.
1961

First Pack Trip

by the steady yet soft footsteps of the horses. From time to time, we would cross small streams of water, where the horses were allowed only a small stop, and then we would move on. I kept a keen eye out for wildlife, but Ted, with his unsurpassed vision in the woods, made most sightings.

By mid-afternoon, we were descending into an area with more dampness and lush undergrowth. The trail was worn, and moisture appeared more frequently. By now the mosquitoes were aware of our presence; they passed on Ted and Francis and took me for fair game. I soon discovered that flailing and swatting were of no use; I submitted and let them have their fill. About this time, the horses started sensing we were about to our destination, Stillwater camp. A few more miles, and the forest started to open to signs of man's handiwork. Trees had been removed discreetly and taken in for log structures, a small smoke house, and a few pieces of rustic furniture. There on a back channel of the Murtle River in a quiet setting sat Stillwater, a place of fishermen's dreams and memories.

In the midst stood a small cabin with a shed porch, just four bunks, stove, and a window. Each time you came, you would go into the nearby woods and collect boughs to soften the sapling slats under your bunk. The second time I visited there, a bear came in the middle of the night, pawed at the door, only to disturb Ted from his slumber. Ted rose from his bunk and picked up a piece of firewood by the stove. He opened the door and struck the bear over the nose. The animal retreated, knowing his next challenge would be met with the rifle.

I would learn forty years later from Ellen that this cabin and eleven others throughout the park comprised Ted's extensive trap line in the winter and spring. Never taking more than one animal per season from any location to preserve the valuable genetic pool and the species, Ted would travel great distances to check on his widely spaced traps.

So we had arrived, having made the trip with no major events. We soon unloaded the horses, put cargo away, and set out food for the evening meal's preparation. We fixed up a nice pot of stew, made from canned venison, vegetables, potatoes and served with homemade bread sent by Jennie. The evening light slowly faded to darkness, and we lit a lantern in the cabin to prepare for the night. Ted told stories of guided trips from the past with slickers from New York who had a tough time in that environment as well as doctors and lawyers who were just as much at home in the wilderness as in the courtroom or surgery wing. Ted finished his bowl of pipe tobacco and proclaimed time for bed. Tomorrow, we would do some carpentry on the porch, collect more wood for the winter, and maybe, just maybe, wet a line. Francis and I were up for that if it took all day to get the jobs done. The lantern went dark, and we faded off to sleep.

I woke up the next morning to some discomfort from the fir boughs on top of the hand-split boards that padded my bunk bed. Certainly an improvement over sleeping on a rocky beach with no air mattress, but that canvas cot on the farmhouse porch was like heaven! I had not traveled all that way, though, to bathe myself in creature comforts. I had an adventure before me, and I was not going to miss a spec of it. Ted had been up for some time and came in the door with a fresh bucket of water. The smell of wood smoke and brewing coffee mixed with the fragrance of the fir boughs on the bunk beds set the stage for a glorious day. Fried eggs, a few fried potatoes, and bacon completed the morning's opening act, and we set off to act two.

Francis and I started by tending to the horses, doling out a bit of grain and water, bringing the wood box up to full, and breaking out the materials we brought for cabin repairs. Ted would be working on some new chimney repairs, the front

*The cabin at Stillwater on the Murtle River.
1959*

door needed a bit of work thanks to grizzly bear visits, and we planned to make some additional camp furniture in the next few days. The forest yielded abundant pieces of downed cedar that could be fashioned into benches, tables, and just about anything you could imagine to keep a hunting and fishing camp well stocked.

That morning, as I explored the edge of the camp and looked at trails leading off to parts unknown, I heard footsteps that vaguely sounded like a horse. I stopped, checked the surrounding woods, and then continued listening till I detected from which direction the sound came. I could vaguely see a less wooded area, maybe a hundred yards off, where more sunlight streamed in. As I started moving in that direction, I was visually ambushed on my left by a moose. My lack of ability to discern the direction of the sound and not really knowing what I had to look for allowed him to move within a hundred feet of me. Of course, that biting taste in my mouth and the momentary paralysis of my entire body left me helpless in the event of an attack, but he seemed more curious than frightened. I stood there and admired his size and distinct features. He was still in velvet and sported what would mature into a rack of antlers suitable for clearing a new road into the wilderness. His large head and shoulders and spindly legs give him an awkward appearance, but their oddly proportioned bodies are adapted to eating water plants from shallow lakes and bogs, fighting for dominance, and breeding. He appeared to have all the necessary equipment to fulfill those god-given missions in life. Having become bored with my lack of desire to engage him, he moved off toward the clearing, which may have had a pond where he could rustle up a noonday meal.

I returned from the mini-adventure, feeling a great sense of discovery, and exclaimed, "I saw a bull moose!"

First Pack Trip

Ted was pleased, but he cautioned, "The moose vill be getting aggressive soon. You vant to be careful ven you are out alone."

At that time in my life, I could hardly fathom why the moose would be "getting aggressive soon." I asked no questions and just assumed the change in moose demeanor must have been due to the seasons or weather.

As the afternoon progressed, we finished up a few projects, and Ted suggested, "I think ve should go out and catch a couple of fish for dinner."

My heart leaped at the announcement. This would be my first experience in the fabled land of GIANT RAINBOW TROUT!

We (I should clarify that, I) scrambled to put things in order, put tools away, round up fishing gear, get the motor out, turn the boat over, and launch it. I stood on the dock impatiently waiting while Ted and Francis casually went about the preparations, occasionally grinning at each other, and exchanging small talk. That dock I spoke of consisted of two enormous cedar logs, roped together, and a few stray boards to walk on, all that was needed to get on the water. At that point, I thought the sun would go down and the moon would be the only light to navigate the log-infested backwater to the fishing grounds by the time my companions joined me. Finally the men arrived, and Ted stepped into the boat, me next, and Francis pushed us clear.

We motored out of the backwater near the camp and up river to another area that was a still water of sorts off the main channel of the Murtle. There were obviously too many in the boat for me to consider casting a fly; the boat measured no more than three and a half feet wide and maybe ten to eleven feet long. It was of an old design but well built and served our purpose of getting to the place where fish of questionable character might be lurking.

I learned later that that was actually the boat that had carried Minnie the packhorse sliding down the hill when she had wandered off the trail with the boat tied to her back. A few strategic repairs were still evident. Several horses had carried boats clear to Murtle Lake, which was twenty-five miles from the farm. It was only about fifteen miles to Stillwater, a mere stone's throw from home.

Quickly the subject of bait took over the topic of conversation. Some suggested that, perhaps, I be put in the water with a rope around my waist and I paddle out as an attractant; when the fish approach, I swim back to the boat close enough that Francis can club one with an oar as I crawl into the boat. A round of laughter exploded across the water and died in the giant cedars that lined the backwater. I, of course, found that sort of verbal torture an attack on my knowledge of the size of trout in those northern woods.

We decided to try a buffet of worms freshly dug at the farm, salmon eggs, and a cast spoon. I cast out a line with a single egg on a bobber and immediately struck pay dirt. The fish, probably topping fifteen inches, jumped wildly and put up a terrific battle. I got him halfway to the boat and, in my nervous state, applied too much pressure, and he pulled the hook. *Amateur*, I berate myself, *these fish are native, not to be played hard. Use a little finesse, give them the space they need, tire them out.*

Ted put on a small silver spoon, cast off near some reed grass, and started a slow retrieve. At first I thought someone had dropped a large rock out of the sky near his pole. No, just a trout the length of his hand and arm to the elbow! I finished poking my eyes back into the sockets as the fish did several more aerial maneuvers and then tired of the fight and headed

First Pack Trip

for the boat. Francis, our official net man, was ready and gently netted the fish but held it in the water and looked quizzically at Ted.

"It von't fit in the pan. Ve'll let it go and catch some smaller vuns."

Now in a total state of shock, I held the net as Francis carefully removed the hook from the fish's jaw, and I lowered the fish into the water. He paused a moment then swam out of the net and leisurely headed for the protection of deeper water.

I was still talking to myself and running through my mind that we had just let a two- to three-pound fish go. *This is one very strange place. I could have taken that fish back to civilization and sold it to some unsuccessful fisherman for a lot of money. He could have had it mounted and told tales of his adventure far north, in the land where they turn lesser fish loose!* I hoped we hadn't jinxed the fish/knife deal and scared the big ones with the knowledge that one of them was going to be mine and it wasn't going back in the water!

We soon returned to fishing and cast our bait to the bottom to stay away from the big ones lurking in the grass. *Lord forbid, we don't want any of those big ones ruining our chance to catch small ones that "vill fit in the pan"!* Only a short time passed, and we were in the money with half a dozen nice sized fish, two apiece for dinner, each probably twelve to fourteen inches.

We left the beauty of that fishing spot, headed back down river, and swung into the backwater of Stillwater camp. The skeletons of cedar and fir trees killed by high water lined the shore and marched into the shallows amongst reed grass.

That land of abundance, still untouched to this day, has been preserved as a provincial park, hopefully, for all time. Years ago, the Honorable A. Wells Gray, Minister of Lands for British Columbia, traveled to that area to view the park to be named after him. It was Ted Helset, a young seasoned hunting and fishing guide, trapper, and woodsman that was chosen to lead him on a small expedition of the area. I hoped Mr. Gray had taken away the memories of his trip as clearly as I had to that point in my summer.

The glow of the evening sun cast long shadows through the trees, and a cool breeze blew as the day stretched to its ending. We decided on a campfire and cooked the fish in a large steel frying pan over a grate. The fish bowed up, they were so fresh. We fried them in the lard from the potatoes, fixed a pot of camp coffee, and ate our fill. I cleaned up after the meal as Ted lit his pipe and told Francis about his trapping in the area and how he came to settle here after his adventures and journey across Canada, how he grew up on the large farm in Norway, and how he eventually met Jennie.

Francis was of native descent, grew up under adverse conditions, and had run into the law on several occasions. He became acquainted with Ted's son when Roy was a guard on a road gang and, through him, came to work for Ted. Francis worked hard and shared folklore and his knowledge of the woods with me. I found him a good resource for what it takes to survive in those parts.

I went over to the small corral and checked on the horses. Ranger was becoming more attached to me and walked to the fence for some personal attention. He moved close that I might pat his neck, rub his forehead, and talk softly to him about the ride home in the next couple of days.

A bit later as we sat by the fire, I pulled out the harmonica I had brought along and did my rendition of "You Are My Sunshine," "Red River Valley," "The Wreck of the Old Ninety-seven," and a few others. The work that day, the meal, the quiet of the evening, the mesmerizing fire, and so many swirling thoughts in my head were taking their toll. Sleep called me to

First Pack Trip

my bunk of fir boughs and sleeping bag. The fire grew dim, and we headed to the cabin.

Ted was up early and moved about the camp. The fire in the stove had taken the chill off the cabin, and fresh coffee alerted my smell to cooked bacon and hot cakes. A man of the woods, hunter, fisherman, horseman, and a darned good cook to boot!

Today we would put a new shake roof on the smoke house and repair a few other shingles on the cabin. On a previous trip, Ted had cut blocks of cedar to fashion shakes for the roof. I got my first lesson on using a mallet and a froe, a flat blade with a wood handle attached at right angles to the blade. Struck with a vine maple mallet of sorts across the wood block, the froe gave wood shakes a half inch thick and thirty inches long. Ted showed me how to work the old shakes loose and weave the new ones into the roof.

My sons, many years later, would benefit from this skill when they earned money cutting cedar into kindling to sell for motorcycle money. They spent the best part of a summer splitting blocks of cedar I had negotiated from a cedar mill that was being torn down and the scrap pile was to be burned. Jerry, the oldest, split the blocks; Erik, the middle son, split the slabs with a hatchet; and Jeff, the little guy, bundled the kindling. It was a team effort, and they worked well together. The whole operation netted them half the money needed to buy their used bikes, and their mom and I filled in the difference.

With the cedar splitting and shake repairs at Stillwater completed, the idea of maybe a few trout to take home for the family was met with excitement.

Ted commented, "You two go get the motor and gear ready. I vill pick up the rest of the tools, and ve'll be off."

Francis and I feverishly gathered up the tackle and motor, Ted finished putting the tools away, and we were ready to go. Ted returned to the cabin and brought his rifle to the boat.

"Why the rifle?" I asked.

Ted replied, "Might see some geese further up. Or maybe ve have to shoot vun of those giant trout you keep asking about! I'm thinking it vould be good if ve could bring a goose home for Jennie to roast."

I had no idea how he planned to shoot a goose with a deer rifle without blowing it to pieces, but he must have had a plan. We shoved off and glided through the still waters and headed up river, the afternoon rays of the sun showing brightly on the surface of the water. We stopped in the area we had fished the other day and picked up some nice trout, two to three pounds, and continued up river a bit. Soon we saw a large sand and gravel bar on the left, and Ted pulled in a ways down river from the bar. He instructed us to hold the boat at the beach, took the rifle, and proceeded up river through the grass and small brush, walking very slowly. He stopped as he approached the crest of the bar. Rifle to his shoulder, he knelt down and took aim. The report from the rifle was deafening, and the air immediately filled with hundreds of geese and the roar of their wings as they flew out of the backwater on the other side of the bar. We could see nothing from our vantage but geese flying overhead—and Ted returning to the boat. He slid the rifle into the boat and hopped in with a smile.

"Let's go see vut ve got!"

I slid the boat off the beach and hopped in. Ted motored up river and swung into the back water. There on the beach lay one lone goose, missing its head. Probably a forty- or fifty-yard shot. The stories of Ted's marksmanship were true, just as I had heard so many times.

First Pack Trip

Goose secured, we head back to the cabin. I cleaned the fish, and Ted gave me a lesson on cleaning birds. After dinner, another fire and more stories.

Ted told us of the time he crossed a river on horseback with one packhorse. It was early winter. He was working his trap line, and hunting season for the guided trips was closed. Two-thirds of the way across the river, a shot rang out from the hillside behind him. The slug hit the water just to his side. He pushed the horse hard to get to the beach, grabbed his rifle from the scabbard, dismounted, and took cover. Soon he spotted two men moving down the hill towards the river. He ordered them to leave their weapons on the other side and cross the river at a shallow point. They approached him with apologies and explained they thought he was a moose (wearing a red and black checked winter coat, of course!). Ted, angry and concerned, took their wallets, discovered they were not local and hunting out of season with no licenses or tags. He confiscated their driver's licenses and explained they would be waiting for them at the ranger station at the entrance to the park. Whether they would stop to pick them up was of no concern; they would be accountable to the authorities for their offenses. The hunters returned back across the river, retrieved their horses, and moved out.

Ted told about one cold early winter morning at the farm. He crawled out of the warm bed to check the day's weather, opened the blind in the bedroom, and looked out on a clear frozen morning. Christmas had come early: Halfway to the hay barn stood a large bull moose. Having not put game away for the season yet, Ted took advantage of his opportunity. Retrieving his rifle from the corner, he quietly slid the window open just enough to get a shot off as Jennie lay peacefully asleep in bed. Most of the report went out the window, but

Jennie cleared the pillow by a sizeable margin. Ted gave her a hug, and apologized, "Ve got meat for the vinter!"

There would be more stories to come in the weeks ahead, some true, some questionable.

The following morning, we got up early and packed up and headed back to the farm. Francis and I prepared the horses and rounded up the camp while Ted loaded the pack boxes and rustled up breakfast. By mid-morning, we had hit the trail, and the mosquitoes were wide awake and enjoying the morning and our company. I played the harmonica as we traveled through the old growth, and Ranger had visions of the pasture and a reunion with his herd. He made his intentions apparent by his constant tugging at the reins, forcing me to pay close attention to keeping him on the trail and preventing him from trying to pass the packhorses.

All too soon, we approached the south end of the park and the gravel road. We passed Ralph and Clara's place. Lippy the moose was in his containment and dashed about in his excitement at seeing the horses. The road curved slowly through stands of aspen and willow, and the north pasture started to appear. The horses now walked with ears up and vocalized a bit to pick up a reaction from the herd. Soon the farm and buildings appeared in view. As we came into full sight, The Two raced through the front yard gate and ran aimlessly around the driveway and hitching rail. Ted got the first hugs, and then Jennie came out and greeted us all while I took charge of hitching the string to the rail.

We gave a brief overview of our trip, presentation of the goose and trout, and then returned to the business of getting the horses out of their gear and into the pasture.

Jim and Ellen had dozens of stories to tell me about how they had spent their time in my absence, helping Mom and trying to keep out of mischief. Roy had taken them on a hike

First Pack Trip

down the creek for a few fish and a dip in the pool up river. I told them how their dad had taught me to make shakes, how the fishing had gone, and how we'd come upon the goose. We spent the rest of the day putting away the tack, drying blankets, and getting the rest of the gear put away. I was now a packer and horseman, becoming more familiar with this life in the north and taking in the vast differences between life in Seattle and life on the trail. In turn, Ted was gaining more confidence in my abilities and bestowed responsibility on me more and more all the time.

While we were gone, Roy had traveled into Clearwater, and I had mail—letters from my sister and brother, Dad and Mom, of course, and one from a girlfriend. She was on a trip with her mom to the East Coast to visit relatives. She was miserable and not having a good time. I felt sorry for her; I was having a blast, and any little bit of homesickness I had felt had vanished by this point. I yearned for even more adventure and sights not yet seen. I still had the knife, and Ted still had the fish to find for me. He regularly would check with me as to whether I had it and was taking proper care of. He really wanted that knife back, and I really wanted that fish!

More Hay!

The last week's pack trip still played fresh on my mind when Ted announced that we would start work on the north hayfield. By now, though, I was getting into shape and was being groomed to run the tractor, as well as riding the hay rake and loading the wagon with the men. Some of the neighbor men would come over to help, and we, in turn, would work on their farms. The work became less exciting and more a regular event with long days and what seemed like short nights. But I found my tolerance for the hard work building, and the days cruised along rapidly. Haying mixed with trips to the swimming hole and constant eating made for a complete day. As much as I ate, I don't think I gained much weight, at least not any fat. Jennie told me she had never seen a boy eat the way I could. But I think she'd forgotten how teenage boys make food disappear. I can imagine she cooked a lot for Roy when he was my age; he was a hard worker as well. By then, the incident of my consuming the twenty-one pancakes was old news; I hit that on a regular basis. It was not uncommon for me to be the last one at the table, cleaning up whatever was left.

I found the afternoons a good time to get away for a while and walk down the road, reflecting about what was changing in my life. I was then about six weeks into the adventure, gaining in strength and knowledge of life on a working farm and working with people who greatly respected the rewards of hard work. I felt a spirit working within me, telling me that I would understand much more of this adventure only in years to come. Now I needed to live the experience; later I would come to know its meaning and how it would tie into the rest of my life.

As time went by, Ted allowed me to take time for a short horseback ride in the area near the farm. Sometimes I saddled Ranger and rode to the park entrance or down the road towards Clearwater. Ranger enjoyed those brief interludes, a bit of lightweight exercise, a chance for us to bond, and quiet time to share alone. He took those non-serious times to test my riding skills and remind me that I rode only as a passenger with his permission, not as the master. He had also turned into a real character that I enjoyed talking to. Like Beeper, the imaginary bird, he never responded but just listened. Only Ranger was a real creature. And he had really developed an appreciation for my harmonica, sometimes walking to the beat of the music—or did I only adjust the tempo?

One afternoon following a long day in the hay fields loading the wagon with Ted and Roy, I took Ranger for a ride down the road towards Clearwater. The day was hot, and I stopped a ways down Hemp Creek and dove in. The water refreshed and restored my senses as I sat by the stream, admiring its meaningless venture through the trees, and grassy areas. I soon felt the heat of the day again and decided to get back on Ranger and take in the breeze riding would generate. A couple of miles further, I encountered a boy about my age. He waved at me as I approached. I got down and introduced myself. He, in turn, introduced himself as Billy Ludtke, a neighbor of the Helsets. We wandered to the side of the road, and found a shady place to tie Ranger while we chatted.

Billy knew of my arrival at the Helsets. I was a bit of a novelty, being from the big city and not knowing anything much about this life in the North Country. He told me a bit about his family, a sister Betty, and life on the farm, as two fifteen-year-olds would describe it. As we stood beside the road slightly above the creek, we engaged ourselves in tossing rocks into the river. As the conversation grew more descriptive and the unspoken question arose of who was the pack leader here, the rock-throwing took on a more serious tone. The rock choices became very specific, as the distance of the throw increased. Now I considered myself a pretty good hurler of stones, but Billy had grown up on this kind of stuff. Soon the distance was approaching critical mass; Billy fired one a long way down river into a large pool. Obviously the only thing I could do was to get one to the other end of the pool, or maybe into the rapids beyond. My rock fell short, and my arm and shoulder would not recover for a couple of days. I admired his strength and appreciated his observation that my rock was probably heavier than his. We spent a bit of time together on several occasions in the weeks to come and enjoyed each other's company.

As the weeks progressed, haying became second nature for me. I had learned many of the tricks and earned more responsibility in the process. Ted, on occasion, would have me mowing and moving the wagon to the hay barn. One day, I was watching the end of the sickle blade, and Ted was driving. We were cutting tall grass south of the farm house, and Jennie's laying hens were running loose in the tall grass. Unseen in the grass, two or three got their legs removed by the mower, and Ted and I scrambled to catch them and put them out of their misery. Upon completion of this task, somewhat stressed, I inquired what we would do now.

"Take the birds to Jennie. She vill fix them for dinner tomorrow night"

That sounded too simple. And, indeed, my presentation of the birds didn't go as smoothly as Ted had given me to believe it would. They were like pets to the dear woman, and my explanation as to the method of their demise was somewhat lame. They were however a terrific addition to the next night's evening meal!

Hay days, good eating, and evenings of working on Mount Stovewood showed in my increasing strength. I had, by then, built the cut pile into a mound bigger than the uncut one. Maybe I had overdone it! Ted and Roy were muttering about the idea of going out for another couple wagon loads of blocks, as it appeared I might get the job done before the end of summer. I never considered that a real threat, based on the tone of their voices. It was similar to the description of the fish you could see under the boat on both sides at the same time. I still employed The Two for stacking wood, but it was getting harder to keep them focused.

Around this time, Jennie and Clara suggested a hike up Pyramid Mountain. It involved a short drive to the trailhead and then a level walk to the base. This was to be an all-day event and to include Clara's two children, Sue and Mike, The Two, and another boy, Stanley Coster. The day burned fiercely, and Pyramid being pretty much treeless, provided no relief from the sun. Jennie and Clara enjoyed the hike at a somewhat normal pace, but I, being of the next generation with the younger kids, took it at quite a different speed.

We speedsters reached the top and discovered that poor Stanley, being not much of a hiker, had fallen behind. Jennie and Clara finally joined us with Stanley in tow. A delicious

*Paul with Jim, Ellen, and cousins & Stanley Coster
1961*

picnic lunch was our reward for conquering that peak (actually a volcanic cinder cone) and another mini adventure was tucked under our belts.

Murtle Lake

Ted announced over dinner (midday meal) one afternoon that a fishing party would be flying into Murtle Lake in a week or so. We would pack in on horseback with provisions a couple of days early and meet them—three businessmen from back east, looking to tangle with some of the best trout fishing in North America. Ted and I would ride in alone with two or three horses and groceries for the stay, along with other material to stock the Murtle Lake cabin. We would meet Ted's clients at Murtle Lake. They would fly in from Kamloops to catch fish and, basically, be taken care of. This is how Ted made his income during those years. He was one of the best and knew how to show his clients a good time with his fishing and hunting abilities, the stories that kept them up half the night, and a game or more of poker and colorful conversation. We could almost guarantee that they would go home with a lot of fish, some of it smoked, and a few trophies for the library wall. Dad caught one of those at Murtle one year, and it still hangs on the wall of our cabin today.

This was to be one of my biggest adventures, time spent alone with Ted, working hand-in-hand, preparing for the trip, going over details, and his constant dialog of trips past, the good and bad ones both. He had a true appreciation for the clients' enthusiasm, always enjoyed their companionship, and gave all the opportunity to have an experience of a lifetime if they so chose.

My job was going to be the camp helper, which would entail hauling baggage, helping with the simple side of meal preparation, and of course not to be forgotten, cleanup. None of this sounded like anything short of another adventure, and I started exercising my brain with all the scenarios that could take place. Possibly this was going to be the trip that would produce the **GIANT TROUT!** I had by now seen some pretty big fish during the previous fishing adventures, but Murtle had a reputation for producing tackle busters.

The time leading up to departure was filled with finishing putting up the recent hay cut and honing my horsemanship. An occasional rabbit hunt kept the mix of good, fresh meat on the table. By now, sleeping on the front porch was my favorite; the upstairs of the farmhouse collected far too much heat in late July and August. A cool breeze and the smell of freshly cut hay wafting over my cot during the night transported me. Adding the regular show of the northern lights over the north pasture to the right of Green Mountain put me as close to Utopia as I could get.

By now I had developed the fondness for this place that would linger forever in my memory. It seemed strange that a place so filled with physical work and daily activity could have such a positive impact on one's emotions. It seemed to go against common sense that hard labor contributed to such good feelings. Though I never stopped thinking about my home in Seattle and the family and friends I missed, this place infected that part of my heart that needed something more than the routine I had experienced until then. Time never stood still there, and the memorable moments stacked up like the firewood I was cutting in my spare time.

As that week progressed, the anticipation of getting back on the trail started taking a firm hold on me. I prepared as much as I could in the absence of the morning of departure—continually going through my bit of gear, sharpening my knife till the blade looked worn and used. My harmonica playing improved, although the list of songs pretty much remained the same. No one ever complained, so I just kept it up, and they seemed to take it in stride.

Finally the night before departure arrived. We had the pack boxes pretty much loaded, and Ted gave me the packhorse attendance sheet. We savored our last home-cooked meal that evening and enjoyed a visit from the Archibalds. They stayed for dinner and brought fresh vegetables from their garden, along with raspberries and shortcake.

Sleep that night did not come easily. I pondered the trip, my home, and how Dad had managed the nights before his travels on this trail. I thought of where my life was headed and what would become of me in years to come. Would I ever come back here and continue on this adventure, or would something else draw me to a different path?

The start of our day came as it always did, before sunrise and the rooster's foretelling of daylight's impending arrival. The morning air possessed a wee bit of chill, and dew hung softly on everything. The horses had moved down the pasture and stood at the fence, knowing that, once again, some of them would get to hit the trail. The main question on their minds was *Who?* The two saddle mounts, Ted's and mine, were at the front and knew, somehow, that we were getting ready.

Following breakfast of my usual ten or twelve pancakes and bacon, we commenced to packing and saddling. It would be a long day on the trail, so Ted was anxious to be gone. The air was becoming sweet with the start of autumn's transformation of the surrounding woods. The leaves were not yet turning but had that special aroma that said fall would be coming shortly.

We set out with three packhorses. I took the rear, being mindful to watch that the packs stayed intact and to call out to Ted if anything started coming apart. We reached the native growth by mid-morning and rode for several hours through stands of trees that had overseen this area for hundreds of years, long before settlers and pioneers had passed by, long before North America had even been inhabited by Europeans. The canopy of the forest blocked out most of the sunlight; only occasional rays spotted the bit of brush that competed for space on the forest floor.

We stopped briefly about noon and had a snack.

Ted asked me, "Do you vant to take the string for avile?"

A big question mark blocked my vision and ability to think. This idea had not even crossed my mind. This was a job for a man, one who knew horses front and back, not some wet-eared city kid who only knew how to ride a bike. Take the string? *Sure!* I was pumped and ready for the challenge. What could happen? Well maybe the horses would take off into the woods, and I'd have to chase them for days or weeks, fight off wild animals, and sleep under the stars.

I finally responded, moved up behind Ted, and away we went. Actually they followed with ease; they knew Ted was up front, and any funny business would be dealt with harshly. It was as much up to Ranger as it was me, and he took on the challenge with an air of authority and leadership. He loved being in the spotlight. *What a ham.*

Later, Ted took back the string as some rougher terrain started developing, and none too soon. We rode through another flat area dotted with those virgin Douglas fir and minimal

*Ted with the pack string
1959*

undergrowth. As we cleared that and the terrain opened up into gentle hillsides and huckleberries, Ted motioned to hold up. He paused for a moment and surveyed the surrounding area, then pulled his rifle from the scabbard. This signaled the hair on the back of my neck to stand erect; something wasn't quite right. My mind processed the possibilities and narrowed it down to a few, centering on the likelihood that something was around us that could cause trouble. Ted motioned me to come forward quietly and not to speak. I moved forward, and he pointed to come up on the left side of the string beside him. As I came to a halt, he pointed to his right up on a gentle rise about one hundred yards ahead—grizzly bear and her cub. A grizzly alone spells a potentially dangerous situation, but add a cub to the mix, and the possible danger escalates. The sow will do anything to protect her offspring.

The light breeze blew in our favor, across and not alerting the bear—or the horses. Ted made his decision.

"You and Ranger hold the string. Keep him in control. I vill move forward, and she vill probably move up the hill to the right. Ven I see that there is not another vun over the rise I vill come back."

He smiled, for what reason I didn't know at the time. For him, this was all in a day's work. I, however, felt a wee petrified. As usual, Ted had the situation well in hand. And he used the opportunity to allow me to learn—to make decisions under unfamiliar conditions, to confront danger, of sorts, to deal with my fears—and to grow. At the time, I knew nothing of that. Instead, I engaged myself in a thought process of the steps needed to get through this and then panicked at my responsibility for tending the string and watching the bear's movements. Only later did I think long enough to fully understand the danger we had been in and what might have happened.

Meanwhile, Ted moved forward, rifle resting across his saddle, and up the trail with confidence and a deep alertness. The bear eventually heard his approach, looked for the cub, and moved out at a good pace. When she was out of sight, Ted moved over the crest, and disappeared. The string seemed oblivious to the entire event, although Ranger did catch the movement of the bear and his hide shivered around his neck, but he stayed in control. Moments later, Ted appeared at the crest and motioned me to move up, as if I had been through events like this hundreds of times. *Where was* my *rifle? And my floppy old hat? And my casual approach to events like this?* All these would come over time; the process of growing to manhood would not deny them to me.

The rest of the trip went without further incident. I played the harmonica, probably thinking that the tunes would alert all the dangerous creatures of the forest of our coming. Ranger liked the sound, wafting his ears in response and keeping rhythm with his pace. We stopped shortly before arriving at Murtle Lake for a break. Ted talked about the bear sighting and commented on my patience and apparent ability to take charge of the string and move through the event with good decisions. Little did he know my heart had beat double time, but he sensed enough to tell me I had done a good job. He shared a few bear stories with me and how unpredictable the creatures can be. Something about Ted, though, told you that when danger reared its ugly head, he always had the upper hand and was in good shape to get you through it. I remember that fondly; he was tattooed with adventure all his life.

Finally an absence of forest ahead of us showed clearly in the sky and signaled our approach to the lake. I could smell the water, clear and crisp in my nostrils, and the coolness in the air. When it came into view, its color showed all its beauty, glistening with a slight breeze, creating sparkles in the sunshine.

Murtle Lake hunting club lodge
1959

Deep sapphire blue, ringed with emerald green forests, it was a stunning sight. Upon reaching the lake, we rode on around the west end and finally arrived at the lodge.

The lodge, affectionately referred to as the Murtle Lake Hunting Club, was a one-room log structure, slept six or eight men, and built in 1937, still stood solid and well cared for. It lay about a hundred feet from the water's edge, where the lake was a bit protected yet deep enough for boats or float planes to navigate. Though large, the lake teemed with fish, and big stringers were always the rule. Dad had pictures in an album at home of his friend Walt, Walt's sons, and Ted at the lodge with stringers of fish two pounds and up. This facility also served as a base camp for a lot of hunting parties Ted guided.

Once we had unpacked, put up the horses, and organized camp, Ted and I settled around a fire. We had fixed a bite of dinner, cleaned up the cabin and prepared for the fishing party to arrive the next day by float plane. Ted politely explained that he would be leaning on me for the week to help out with camp chores, helping the men get around, probably cleaning a hell of a lot of fish, and keeping the smokehouse going. None of the above did anything but get me wired for the activities to come. We had our evening coffee, and I played the harmonica. I think Ted was growing yet wearier of "Red Sails in the Sunset," "You Are My Sunshine," and "The Wreck of the Old Ninety-seven." He really had no choice though. Music stores were scarce in those parts; besides I was the only musician!

Weariness finally overtook the both of us. Off to the bunks we went for a good night's sleep.

Morning brought the usual spectacle of sun rising in the east and lighting up the lake with jewel-like sparkles on its surface, as a very gentle breeze came up. After our breakfast, I fed and watered the horses and loaded wood in for the cook stove, and we turned the boats over and got the camp ready for our guests. I was impatient for them to arrive, minutes turning into hours it seemed, and no sign of them. It was about the time I felt as if we had been stood up when a very far-off sound of a plane engine grabbed me. I looked up in the eastern sky and watched as a small plane passed over the east end of the lake and disappeared into the northern sky. They must be lost, I thought. *Hello? We're right here, guys!* Another hour passed, and I tried not to show my anxiety. Then suddenly a plane seemed to drop out of the tree tops behind us and descend to the lake's surface. It hesitated just above the water for what seemed like an eternity and then gracefully set down on the pristine waters. The craft was a De Haviland Beaver 1, a ruggedly built Canadian plane, just right for getting into the back country, whether on water, snow, or runway. The plane turned around after landing and taxied down the lake to the lodge. The engine had a throaty roar to it, very authoritative, and made me feel as if it could carry anything out of here, fish, moose, bear, or all three at the same time.

The Pilot eased the plane up to a couple of logs with boards nailed onto them, which served as a floating dock. When he had killed the engine, the door opened, and out stepped our guests. Three gentlemen of various ages, nicely dressed for the occasion, and appearing quite excited about what was to come. Ted shook hands with one man first and then was introduced to the other two, whom he had not met before. They were, indeed, from the East Coast. When we had all exchanged greetings, the pilot and I were put in charge of unloading their gear, and I proceeded hauling it to the lodge. The men offered to help, but Ted generously put them off.

"No, Paul vill get the gear. You men come on up; fix yourselves a drink. I'll get lunch started!"

Yes, Paul vill get the gear. The plane had a payload capacity of two thousand pounds. I don't know how the pilot got it up in the air. Those guys brought tons of food, alcohol, enough clothing to change three times a day for the next week, oh, and fishing gear,… Don't get me started.

Once the pilot and I got everything out, we went up, and joined the men for lunch. Ted and one of the men who seemed to enjoy the kitchen aspect of this operation fixed soup and sandwiches for everyone. Ted just kind of showed him where everything was. I could see this guy was going to inherit the chef's hat! Once we had eaten, the pilot said his good-byes and got into the plane. We untied him and pushed him around to head out. The engine jumped to life and slowly got its rhythm. He taxied out onto the lake and, with a roar of the engine, took off down lake and slowly rose up and banked south over the trees. He was headed back to Kamloops and would return in five days.

The guests spent the next few hours stowing their gear, rolling out sleeping bags, assembling fishing gear, and visiting. Ted included me in the conversations, introducing me as summer help, up from Seattle, whose dad was a client and had left me here for the summer.

They were envious of me in that I had gotten the opportunity to sign on with such an incredible situation. I would review the label "incredible situation" at the end of the week after cleaning their two hundred or so fish and reloading their two thousand pounds of gear. All three men had sons and compared me favorably to their boys in my ability to converse and eagerness to work and handle the chores. I presumed their sons had a privileged lifestyle and were more in line to succeed in business than to work in a fish camp. I liked my situation and would later in life praise my father for giving me the work ethic, which I would pledge allegiance to my entire adult life.

As the afternoon approached, Ted organized the men into two boats. He would take two of the men, and I would go with the fellow who had been here several times. He and I hit it off from the start. I'll call him John, nice man, and he was one heck of a fisherman. We loaded into the two boats and headed out on the lake to one of Ted's good spots. The fishing on Murtle was primarily trolling, using spoons or flatfish. Both worked well, although some liked the pop gear and worms. John liked the back waters and fishing with flies, my kind of guy. He was good at it, could thread a fly right where he wanted it and got incredible results. Over that week, I got some good pointers on fly fishing, and he enjoyed watching me progress. By the time evening fell that first day, we had struck it rich with fish. The two men in the boat with Ted had never seen fishing like this in their lives. Ted was grinning from ear to ear, knowing the week was off to a good start and he had me to help that he might spend more time with his clients and not clean thirty fish at a time. Although, as I found out, they go fast once you get the hang of it.

Before dinner, there were rounds of drinks for the clients. Ted partook on a minimal basis, keeping his head about him for whatever might arise in or out of camp. By the time dinner was through, I had done the dishes, built a bonfire, put all the little fishes in the cooler box, straightened up, and it was break time for me, as the men sat by the fire and listened to the stories, eyes as big as saucers. One thing Ted could do was tell a campfire story that you weren't going to forget for the rest of your life. Surprisingly, 75 to 80 percent of it was true; a little embellishing was just good for the soul and made the story even more exciting.

I waited that first night to see how long those guys could hold up after such an eventful day. They were troopers, but the promise of a pre-sunrise start to the fishing soon had them thinking about hitting the sack. I was thankful they were done. I was tired, really tired, and we had only begun the week. Tomorrow would bring a full day of fishing and getting the smoke house started.

First morning for the group brought out some complaints about the early hour. But I had the fire stoked and coffee going by the time the last one was up, and Ted was down at the lake, readying the boats and gear. The one fellow that liked to cook, let's call him Leonard, was soon juggling his pots and pans and getting breakfast going. Ted returned from the beach and poured himself a cup of coffee. He praised Leonard for his heroic efforts at getting breakfast going and told the men I was continually poisoning him with my cooking. I never so much as lifted a pan the entire summer! Ted was the camp cook supreme. Jennie, of course, never let him in her kitchen; that's a whole different kind of food preparation!

Ted sat down on a bench at the table and declared, "Ve had a bear through the camp last night. I heard him. He didn't find anything to get into. Let's keep all food picked up. He von't bother us."

The two first-timers asked what kind of bear it was. Ted told them a grizzly, pretty good size. I told the men that Ted had his rifle with him, but had forgotten to bring any cartridges. Ted explained he would use me for bait and strangle it with his bare hands, so not to worry.

Following breakfast, we loaded up and shoved off for a morning of fishing. Ted, the other new fellow, let's call him Bill, and I took one boat; Leonard and John took the other. I got a line in the water, Bill followed, and Ted ran the motor, telling fish stories that often zigzagged over the line between fact and fiction. Fishing was good that day, and everyone got into good action. They focused on the bigger fish and saved their limits for later in the week. By eleven, they had had their fill. Back at camp, I cleaned the catch and prepared them for smoking while Ted got the brine ready and got them soaking. The smokehouse was a fairly sizeable structure, and the fish were put on cedar racks or hung. Eight to twelve good hours of alder smoke rendered them fit for eating. These would be kept cool for the trip home, with ice brought in on the plane.

That evening after supper, the men stayed up playing poker and enjoying their share of the liquor they had brought with them.

I sat outside at the fire, played my harmonica, and reflected on the day's activities. This triggered thoughts of home, how far away it was, and what everyone was up to. I had not written anyone for a while and looked forward to doing that when we got back to the farm at Hemp Creek. Then I thought farther back, about all the things I could recall in my short lifetime to this point—the time spent with my parents, Mom with her troubles and how she had bravely dealt with them as best she could, Dad the perpetual workaholic, always pursuing his career to keep the best he could offer in front of us.

I had a comfortable life, yet I felt there was something missing. Exactly what, I didn't know; perhaps it would come to me. I gave it very little thought at the time.

Returning to the lodge, I saw the poker was getting serious. I asked Ted if he still had his knife.

He laughed, "Yes, and I vill have my old vun back before you leave for home this fall!"

I turned in and fell sound asleep, thinking about the knife and the deal Dad had struck with Ted before he left. Was the giant trout to be a reality?

The following morning found our guests not so quick on the draw. The late night had rendered them somewhat reluctant to get the intended early start on fishing. Ted and I got some breakfast going, and the smells of coffee and bacon cooking did the trick. Two of them rose, like spirits out of the grave. John, the fly fisherman, was out the door after breakfast and trying his luck in the nearby shallows. He was a true sportsman, also hunted up there some years and had good luck with Ted as a guide.

When John returned, it was decided that he and Bill would go out that morning, and I would stay back with Leonard, the cook. He was having some difficulty getting started that morning, and opted to work on an elaborate pot of stew for supper that evening. Meanwhile, Leonard returned to his bunk for the morning. I was fine with the plan. I knew that the other two men were excited for a day spent with one of British Columbia's best fishing guides and storytellers. The men took lunches so would not be back till three or so. Ted had suggested that they go through the passage and try their luck on Diamond Lake.

After feeding and watering the horses, picking up the camp area, and splitting up a jag of wood, I settled down against a rock near the shore. Last night's thoughts about home and my life were still with me; I needed some time to reflect.

My brother Carl, six years older than I, had not been my best companion. He had been abusive with me verbally and physically, beyond what could be called sibling rivalry. As a boy, I had quickly learned to steer a wide berth around him. He had constant battles with my dad to the age of eighteen, at which point he dropped out of high school, and Dad ordered him into the Air Force. Although I didn't lack for friends my age, the pressures exerted by Carl and Dad's need to take time with him, at times, deprived me of the family structure I needed. Dad did a great job of supplying me with boyhood experiences, Cub and Boy Scouts, trips alone, fishing, and of course, Hemp Creek farm

But I needed more. I was looking for guidance from a higher authority, possibly someone that superseded my father and anyone else connected with my life. I had not yet experienced a true spiritual connection nor did I even know what that meant, let alone realize that I yearned for it. A few years later, at seventeen, I joined the Catholic Church, looking for that special relationship with God. But I had made only a religious connection—saying specific prayers, going to church, and attending to other established obligations of the faith. I would not learn anything about the subtle differences between religion and spirituality till I was sixty. Nor would I accept or ask the Lord to come into my heart till that time. So, at fifteen, I lived in confusion on which voice to follow.

I sat against that rock, my mind occupied with the direction of my life, looking out on the beauty of Murtle Lake, and I seemed to hear a voice talking to me, as though it was detached, not me talking to myself. It seemed to be building me up, telling me I was all right, and that my strength would see me through the years ahead. I would have greater challenges than Carl or school, and I would be strong.

The voice spoke true. The years ahead did prove challenging, yet something or someone always led me on. I first gave credit to myself that my early life's experiences made me as tough as Dad said he wanted me to be. Dad gave me all sorts of prescriptions along that line: "Be yourself." "No one's going to do your job for you." "When the going gets tough, the tough get going." "I don't get ulcers; I give them." Those seemed like good examples to follow. After all, they came from Dad, and he knew all there was to know. What else was there? Yet this other voice that spoke to me was soft, always seemed supportive, loving, and genuinely concerned. But I didn't look in the right location for the source. I thought it was I, telling myself

Dad at Murtle lake 1959

the situation was all right, I could do whatever came my way, I was going to make it. No, only later I learned that the voice came not from my head or my mind; it came from the Lord, speaking to my heart.

Those messages and the voice would come to me many times as I grew older, but never did I interpret their origin till I came to the Lord. It was then that the remembrance of the power of the experience that summer day when I sat by the lake, along with numerous other times, made me realize he had always been with me, since my birth, holding me fast, bringing me safely through all my years finally to connect me with his love for me and the true understanding that I was his beloved son. This fuller understanding escaped me on the beach that day, but my heart experienced a tremendous joyfulness as I felt loved and comforted and assured of the goodness within me. I needed that.

Some time later that day, Leonard came down looking for me. He wanted help in the lodge finding fixings for the evening meal and a little company. Leonard abandoned himself to his stew and clearly enjoyed indulging in that side of his creativity, pondering over his spices and having me sample each addition. We shared a little bit about our lives, where we had been, and what ambitions I held. That was a tough one, so I winged it about wanting to study architecture or maybe build boats. Neither of those would happen if I did not figure out why school was such a burden for me. I was content just to get by, sometimes falling short of even that lowly goal. Leonard was an attorney, corporate I believe, well spoken, and like me, a true jabber box. He enjoyed the outdoors but was not a purist. He most of all liked the camaraderie with the guys and the adventure of being away from the big city.

Around mid-afternoon, we heard the boat coming into the cove, Ted at the helm, Bill and John with big grins on their faces. This could only mean one thing: They had GIANT TROUT! They really did. John had one close to twenty-three inches, Bill had two that cleared twenty. These would be treated specially so that that they could be mounted on their return home. Everyone was excited, lots of hand shaking, thumping of chests, lies about the ones that got away, and of course, "Let's go celebrate!" Following rounds of chilled beverages, Leonard and I got things ready for the evening supper. His stew was a work of art, acknowledged even by Ted, who suggested that Jennie would probably like his recipe. I rather doubted that; she could cook the socks off this guy, probably did her first stew before she gave up dolls.

Once again the evening went late, more conversation and then cards. As the night air cooled, we retired to the fire outdoors, drank coffee, and Ted told stories about hunting and trapping trips from years past. John asked Ted to tell his friends more about the accident and survival story, and Ted obliged, telling of his determination to get back to his family and Jennie, that he never gave up hope, even when he started losing consciousness. To this day, I have spent time and been in the presence of men of character, but none carried it so well, and certainly none shared of their time and talents as did Ted Helset. I would think of him regularly in years to come and use him as a guidepost, only regretting that I had not spent more time with him years later.

The fire was dying, eyes were getting heavy, and bed seemed like a good option. Morning would come early, and activity would fill the day—smoking of fish, packing, and getting the guests' fish ready for the trip home.

I woke early that morning, feeling somewhat accomplished in that I had done a lot over the last few days. Murtle

Ted with a client Murtle Lake
1959

Lake truly was a beautiful place, only to be outdone by the quality of the fishing and enhanced by the combination of good people, conversation, and food cooked out of necessity, not excess. The morning went fast, breakfast, coffee, and more reflecting by all the men, each sharing his stories of adventures gone by and what the future held. They always included me in the exchanges, but my pint-size adventures and lofty goals seemed inconsequential by comparison. Who was I kidding? I didn't really know what my future held; I was living the moment, and that seemed good enough. At that point, who'd want more than riding horses, shooting rabbits, catching giant trout, and sleeping under the stars in central British Columbia? Only a fool would want more than that, or so I thought at the time.

Ted spent the morning preparing a lot of the fish for smoking, and I busied myself getting together what I could for the trip out tomorrow. Everyone kept busy. The guests worked on a combination of pulling their gear together, doing a bit more fishing, taking pictures of everything under the sun, and catching up on a bit of napping. Ted and I kept the smokehouse going all that day, Leonard fixed dinner and supper, and John and Bill finished rounding up all the gear and getting it stacked in the lodge. We would clean up the cabin that night and only cook breakfast before breaking camp the next morning. As the day progressed, the conversations grew quieter, all knowing that their trip was almost over for them and we would probably never see each other again as a group. I was excited to get back to the farm, see The Two and the rest of the family, and catch up on some writing to family back home. The trip had been a 100-percent success—no accidents, everyone got fish, and we all enjoyed each other's company.

The following morning, we fixed and finished breakfast and did the last bit of packing. The Beaver showed up about eight, taking its landing in from the east. It touched down gracefully and proceeded across the water to our location. The pilot maneuvered it to the floating log dock and killed the engine then stepped out onto the pontoon and threw a line to the men. The plane's arrival signaled the start of much activity, especially for me—get the gear to the beach and, of course, the fish. I started lugging bags down, and Ted got the fish boxes to the beach. The pilot carefully loaded the plane so it was properly balanced and, I guessed, would fly straight! When we had loaded and secured everything, we all had a round of hand-shaking and good-byes. Back in the sixties, men didn't hug, just did maybe a bit of brisk chest-thumping. But whatever the gestures, they indicated the obvious—people would miss people. I was pleased that they had had a good time and Ted had another successful guide trip under his belt, and a few bucks.

The men climbed aboard, and the door closed. Ted and I cast off the lines and gave the plane a good push around. Once again, the propeller turned several times, and the engine exploded to life. After taxiing down lake, the plane turned around and headed back our way full throttle. At the last minute, it rose off the water and sailed over the trees behind us and soon was out of earshot. I stood there a moment, wondering if I would hear it again in the distance, then realized Ted no longer stood with me. That man missed his wife and family and wanted to waste no time in heading back home: He was already moving horses to the hitching rail and getting ready to pack up.

We spent the morning saddling and loading the horses and making up the cabin, and soon were ready to hit the trail. We were a little bit lighter going back, what with the gear we had brought for the lodge and groceries we had consumed. The horses seemed more than ready to get back to the farm and the rest of the herd. Ranger took a few miles to get the idea in his head that I was directing the pace and direction we would go. He acted like he knew a short cut; I wasn't buying into it. Ted's horse knew better than to strike out on his own; the consequences would be painful at the least.

Murtle Lake stayed with me for a long time. Its beauty, together with the remoteness, gave it a feeling of tranquility and peace. It was incredible that such a scene of beauty had been seen by only a handful of people over the years. But soon the highway would pass close by, and later, a road would be developed right to its shores. Its secrets up to that day, though, would remain in the hearts of only a few of us.

Ted had been one of the first guides to work this part of the Canadian wilderness and had cabins scattered all through the area. When the government designated the area a provincial park, he made himself available to those charged with managing the area and, in the years to come, gave of himself that the wildlife would flourish and not be taken over by excessive hunting and fishing. In recent years, I have looked online and found his name mentioned in wildlife research conducted by the government, including helping to keep statistics on the health of the moose population. And he remained the premier guide in the area, and officials looked to him as the go-to person for information about many aspects of Wells Gray Provincial Park.

We had started on the trail in the morning but not as early as on the trip up.

At a break, Ted commented, "Ve can stop for the night if you get tired, or ride till dusk, which should have us to the farm before dark."

I opted for a ride straight through. I missed the farm and longed for my bed on the porch, or even upstairs with The Two. The miles wore on. We stopped briefly, on occasion, to give the horses a bit of water at a stream crossing or just to rest for a moment. Ted seemed tireless; I was feeling a bit of saddle fatigue but wanted to press on. As the afternoon wore late and the shadows stretched out longer, the light started fading in the deeper parts of the forest. Wildlife was starting to move about, lots of deer and occasionally a moose could be heard in the distance. I was wary of another bear encounter, but we lucked out on the trip back.

As dusk started setting in, the horses seemed to want to pick up the pace; they knew we were getting closer to the road, and sure enough not long after, there it was; the highway home. We turned down the road and followed it a few miles till we came to the entrance of the park and Ralph and Clara's place. They had heard us approaching and were standing out at the road when we arrived. We got off and exchanged greetings. They were glad to see us home and safe, told us everything was good down at the farm and Jennie was waiting, figuring we would try to get there that evening. We said goodnight and headed on down the road.

As we made the last turn, and the lamplight in the windows appeared, we heard Trixie and Fenris, the elkhounds, announcing our arrival in the valley. Before we closed the distance to the farmhouse, The Two exploded out the door and ran up the road to greet us. Ellen ran to her dad, and he reached down and grabbed her hands and pulled her up onto the saddle. Jim climbed up my leg, and I somehow helped him wrestle his way behind me on the back of the horse. We all rode the rest of the way down the road and to the hitching rail in front of the house. A lot of laughing, cheering, and running about ensued, as Jennie came out, exchanged a hug with Ted, and the kids all talked at the same time, telling about their week alone at home.

Murtle Lake

Following the greetings and latest news of the area, it was apparent Ted and I still had a lot of work to do—unpacking, breaking down the horses and getting them into the pasture, putting away most of the gear and tack, and cleaning up a bit for a late supper and more conversation.

Ted summarized the trip as a success and added, "Paul vuz a good svamper, helping vith the clients, and cleaned lots of fish!"

My head swelled up with pride that Ted should offer such observations about my performance. He told about our encounter with Mother Bear and her cub and how I pulled the pack string. The Two told about visitors throughout the week and how Mom had taken them up to the pool on Hemp Creek and they had displayed their swimming skills. Little Harold was still a tiny infant at this time so had little to offer about how he had spent the week.

Jennie told Ted that the Ludtkes wondered if we might be able to come over for a few days and help with haying. He thought that would work out fine. I would get a chance to visit with Billie and his sister Betty, both about my age, and share stories about the big city with them. We all helped clean up, said our good-nights, and headed off to bed.

The Two insisted I sleep up with them that night. I agreed, conditional to silence for the rest of the evening and conversation again only in the morning. That was a futile request. They bent my ear well into the night, as I fell off to sleep.

Back Home on the Farm

Morning brought a cloudy day, not terribly cool, but a break from the heat of the last few weeks. Following chores and a bit of time on the woodpile, Ted suggested we drive over to the Ludtkes and see how the haying was coming along. The Two piled into the truck, I rode in the back, and we headed down the road a ways. They had most of their hay cut and some coiled. We talked with Charlie and agreed to spend a few days over there helping. I would work full-time, and Ted would put in as much time as he could, but he had other duties at home to tend to as well. I stayed there for the day while Ted took The Two home and joined me later, along with Billie and another helper. We finished coiling and stacking most of the hay in the next day, and the weather came back sunny. Within four or five days, we had most of it in the barns, and Charlie thanked us, saying he and the boys would finish up.

I spent those few days, on occasion, visiting with Billie and Betty. She was a pleasant girl; I enjoyed her company, and I felt flattered that she seemed to like me. During that week on the days that I went alone, I would saddle up Ranger and ride to the Ludtkes. On the return trip, they would saddle up their own mounts and ride back with me. It wasn't a terribly long distance, but I enjoyed the company, and the horses enjoyed the exercise.

Our own hay was pretty well finished. Ted and I spent the next two weeks finishing up a couple of spots both north and south and worked on fences again. I spent any off-time and early morning and evening busting away at the woodpile. By then, I had a method down for busting up those thirty-inch-round spruce blocks. I was slowly closing in on the door of the woodshed with row after row of firewood. The splitting, at that point, had become mostly a consumer of time and not energy. My arms responded without complaint to the work not only there but all around the farm.

Following our return from Murtle Lake, I had received mail from home—letters from my sister, Mom, and two from Dad. I think he was starting to miss me, wondering if I might not come back! He wanted to know if Ted had his hunting knife back yet. I wrote him, no, I didn't have the giant yet!" Mom wrote me, said all was well with her, she missed me, the dog and the cat missed me too. It seemed as if everyone missed me, but the homesick bug hadn't bitten me yet. True, I was missing some of the relationships, but the pace of activity and the constant work and trips out did not allow much time for reflection of what was going on at home. That would all have to wait.

Hemp Creek always beckoned with its endless supply of fish for catch-and-release. The pool above the farm tempted me on any hot day. And, of course, the horses constantly needed tending to. Sometimes, Jim, Ellen, and I even found time to do a little bit of exploring in the nearby woods. But whenever Ted noticed I had too much time on my hands, he always found a good chore for me—helping shoe a horse, fix tack, sharpen tools, shoot a couple of rabbits for dinner, or help Jennie when she had a job that needed an extra set of hands.

Soon after, Ted and I took a couple of men who had driven to the farm to Stillwater for a few days of fishing. They were hunters from the States and would be back in the fall for moose and bear. But because they knew the fishing was excellent at Stillwater, they wanted to come up while the weather was still good. The trip went well, and I found myself falling into the routine of getting the horses ready, helping out around the camp, and just being available when something needed doing.

When we returned to the farm, Ted noted to Jennie that the wild huckleberries near Stillwater were getting ripe and that we should go for a pick in another week. The trip was made by The Two, Jennie, Ted, and of course, good old me. The Two could not ride by themselves, so they rode double with us. The total purpose of this trip was for berry picking, wild Canadian huckleberries, dark purple, and sweet as honey. Smaller than a blueberry but similar in flavor, it took a lot of them to fill a pail. Once camp was established, all of us fanned out in an area near Stillwater and picked berries. The Two consumed their part of the picking and dropped one in the pail from time to time as an offering to the huckleberry Queen, Jennie that is. Ted and I fell off the trail of the wild huckleberry first and found chores to do around camp. We finished up the roof of the cabin, fixed the stovepipe, and busied ourselves with odd jobs.

We kept a close eye on Jennie and the kids. Ted was wary of bears now that the berries were getting ripe; they would be moving in for their share. He had already noticed bear scat along the trail containing lots of purple color. Indications of bears in the vicinity would be great in another month and a half when hunting season arrived, but not now with the family around. It took Jennie about two days with the kids helping and Ted and me lending a hand to get her quota, about four five-gallon containers nearly full. She would put some up and trade the rest around the Clearwater valley.

Years later I would reflect on this event when watching my wife pick the little wild blackberries that grew in the woods near our home. She, too, was a berry-picking queen. With our three sons in tow, she would attack the fields of strawberries and raspberries and fill her pails.

We returned from this trip, and Jennie found homes for all her hard work. She truly was a remarkable woman, always had the energy to complete any number of tasks, kept us all in clean clothes, fed us delicious, sumptuous meals, and always had time to listen. The load must have exhausted her on numerous occasions, but she never showed it. I marveled at how both she and Ted could keep up the pace. It was the survival instinct in the both of them. Even though the demands of the farm never let up, they had relative comfort. It had not always been so, especially when they had first moved down to the area and settled the farm, cleared land, built all the buildings, raised the first two children, and carved out a living. Their obvious determination caught my attention and reinforced what I had seen in my Dad all those years. I understood now why he was so enamored with Ted and Jennie. They were a team, afraid only of not surviving, and worked together to fulfill the mission: create a home, raise the children, and send them off independent but connected as a family.

That togetherness was seriously lacking in my family. It had collapsed years ago, when I was just a small child. The environment we lived in didn't support a family staying together and working as a team. To achieve financial success, Dad slaved at his job, almost as though he enjoyed the time away from the turmoil that persisted around the house. Mom had serious problems, my brother was out of control, and I just kept out of the way.

But up at the Helsets' home, I saw a whole new way of living where people had a true sense of family, working and playing together because they had a common goal—to survive, make something of the situation, move on to the next step, never sell themselves short. I didn't witness a lot of religion or spirituality within their family that summer, but their daily actions showed that they were connected with the Lord through nature and human bonds. Spirituality takes many forms, not always outward, and manifests itself in people's interactions, their showing concern and respect for each other, and their sense of right and wrong.

Summer was slowly coming to a close. The air gave a hint that summer was growing tired of warm days, the growing vegetation had reached its peak, and people started making subtle preparations for fall and winter. We had finished the haying, and I had managed to avoid having my feet cut off or being skewered by the hay rake. The blisters from the rake lever had matured into skin that resembled the back of a rhinoceros. And I was reaching the point of completion with the woodpile. Ted was obviously amused that I had stuck with it. Rows and rows of neatly stacked stove wood reached the roof of the shed. Outside, the splinters of chopping littered the ground, and the splitting block looked the worse for wear. But the most noticeable change was the absence of the block pile that at one time had blocked my view of the mountain behind. During the summer, I always feared that Ted and Roy would get it in their heads to replace the pile beyond the one they had added to earlier on.

We sat at the supper table one evening, enjoying the meal and bits of conversation. Ted finished his food and pushed his plate ahead to accommodate his folded arms on the table.

He looked at me with contemplation, kind of sizing me up and debating something in his mind. I prepared myself for an order to go out and fulfill some sort of task involving enormous amounts of physical energy and, probably, sleep deprivation. No, I'd completely misjudged.

"So, do you still have my knife?"

I had waited for that question all summer. Like a lit fuse, I replied, "I have the knife. What I need is a really big fish."

"Vell, I know of a place at Stillvater. It might take us a few days. Ve can leave tomorrow, and be back by the veekend. The family that's staying in the cabin is leaving back to New Vestminster the following veekend. You can catch a ride home vith them, and they vill put you on the bus for Seattle."

I probably sat there for no more than a few seconds, but the time played out in my head as hours or days. The hunt for the giant trout was now in my sights; home was shortly behind that. My mind wandered off to all that had happened during the summer, my adventures, discoveries, time spent with all the people I had met, the stories that never ended. Would I remember half of them when my children came along? I recognized a sense of growth within me. I was no longer a boy; growing up had finally found its mark. The ensuing years would add to my growing to manhood, but I finally had a good start on it. I had overcome indecision and fear of the unknown, I had taken responsibility and accepted the cards dealt me, and I had made a closer connection to something that still was not clear in my mind, a relationship with something greater than all that. The time was coming when I would be drawn to church to further my understanding of God and his beloved son Jesus Christ. And many years after that, I would begin a walk with the Lord, invite him into my heart, and allow him to live through me.

Back Home on the Farm

I set those thoughts aside, and only one thing ran over and over in my mind: Where was that fish?

The evening concluded with talk of home and my family, a kind of refresher for what lay ahead, that I'd complete the summer, but I had a life after that. Ted and Jennie seemed pleased that the summer had gone well. I was, at that point, still in possession of all my arms and legs, I'd survived the fall out of the hayloft with nothing but a puncture through my arm, and the tetanus present on the farm seemed to have warded off infection. Ranger had kept me busy yet at the same time tutored me on the dos and don'ts of good horsemanship.

That night I slept upstairs with The Two. We stayed up late, talking of our adventures and what would become of us in years to come. Both had grandiose visions of the future. I was hardly in touch with what mine held, but I did know that I hoped we would stay connected.

We finally all fell off to sleep, only to be what seemed like immediately awakened by the first rays of daylight and the rooster.

That day, Ted realized a few things still needed attending to before we could leave, so we put off the trip to Stillwater till the next morning, and we would leave early. I sorted through my gear and assembled what I thought I would need, checking all my tackle and puzzling over what this giant trout might want presented to it.

The Two were excited for me and remained close by my side the entire day. We put in a few more hours on the woodpile, helped Jennie with some of the chores, and spent the day pretty much at leisure. Later in the day, Ted and I assembled what tack we would need for the morning and went over what other gear we would take. Ted got out his rifle that evening, cleaned it, and got the 22 out and checked it over.

"Ve vill take this, maybe see a grouse or two for our supper. I'll put a scabbard on your saddle. You can carry it."

A rifle on my saddle! Hunting! And fishing for the GIANT TROUT! Oh my word!

That night I slept on the porch with the northern lights peeking over the trees up the pasture. The air now carried a chill that foretold of a season slowly coming to a close. I could feel this summer being indelibly printed on my heart, and there was still one chapter to be written. I hoped that I knew the ending; I could only pray at this point.

In Pursuit of the GIANT TROUT

We both beat the arrival of daylight by at least an hour. I was up and dressed by the time the front door opened. Ted just grinned and said nothing. Jennie, as was customary, was already in the kitchen, preparing a bit of breakfast for the two of us.

While Ted started assembling gear, I stole up into the upper pasture and rounded up our horses and two packers. Breakfast was a quiet affair, but you could have cut the air with a knife around my chair. I was almost to the point of making myself sick, yet tried to come off with the composure that befitted a seasoned packer, hunter, fisherman, man of the woods, adventurer, all that kind of stuff.

Jennie inquired, "So are you getting a little homesick yet Paul?"

I replied that I'd been thinking about home a bit more in the last few days but was excited about Ted's and my fishing trip. Ted, attempting to be serious, inquired as to the disposition of the knife. I replied it was packed in my gear, ready to be returned to its true owner. He mumbled something, apparently satisfied that the deal was still on. He was playing this knife thing out to the hilt and, constantly throughout the summer, had talked up the fish and questioned me as to my ability to get it to the boat.

After breakfast, we finished packing and prepared to head out. The Two were up now and lingered around the horses and preparations. Ted brought out the two rifles and handed me the 22. I slid it into the scabbard as though I'd done it hundreds of times. I was able to accomplish this by having done it that many times in my head during the mostly sleepless night. We exchanged our good-byes with Jennie, The Two, and little Harold. Ted swung up onto his big black mount, and I handed him the pack string. I mounted up on Ranger, turned, and headed up the road behind the string. One last look and a wave, and we were off. Trixie and Fenris barked us a farewell as we moved out, running up the side of the road a ways before turning back.

We passed by Ralph and Clara's place. Calypso was in his pen. He'd been chasing cars of late, so he was in time out. It appeared they were both gone, so we didn't stop or whistle. As we continued to ride, the coolness of the morning refreshed the horses, who enjoyed the time on the trail and the exercise. Ranger had an unusual alertness about him and seemed spirited about the trip. Perhaps he sensed the upcoming hunting season where he would put in many hours on the trail and get lots of attention.

We moved in and out of the large stands of native growth timber that blocked out all traces of sunlight. The starkness of their giant trunks and the absence of anything else growing, save an occasional fern, gave the landscape a real sense of power and strength. That was one of nature's most prominent displays, a true sense of time and absence of man's intervention and destruction. I cherish the memory of that ride through Gods beauty as though it was yesterday.

As usual, we stopped occasionally for the horses to get a brief sip out of the creek, then continued on. Ted, head and eyes constantly moving, kept a sharp lookout for game and signs of their numbers. He operated not out of fear but to assess the fall's hunting prospects. The abundance of game or lack thereof would play heavily on the success of his business in the coming months and through the next years. As a conservationist, he never took game recklessly but killed only what the area could afford in order to sustain a healthy population. Through observation on trips such as our, he knew where animals were in numbers and where not to take any till they had recovered.

At one of our stream crossings, we spotted a covey of grouse as they flew up off the ground and perched in some vine maple. Ted pulled up and turned around, gave me the thumbs up and indicated two. I dismounted and tied Ranger off to a small branch, even though he was trained not to move more than five feet if his reins were on the ground. I took the 22 out of the scabbard and moved off the trail and closer to the birds. Using a convenient log as a rest, I took my time and squeezed off each shot carefully. The years of practice with Dad out at the property we used to have paid off: two for two, good clean shots. I fetched the birds and took them to Ted. He put them in the back of his game jacket, and we continued on. I was feeling pretty darned good but kept it to myself. I know Ted was having a good time, mentoring and just maybe re-experiencing some of his first adventures. He didn't engage in big celebrations for achievements; he knew accomplishment was a part of the whole growing-up experience, a necessity as opposed to something warranting a treat or printed award or trophy.

As the day wore on, the sun's rays would occasionally find their way through the woods and play on the leaves of poplar, vine maple, and huckleberries. The colors were mostly green still, but shades of yellow and orange were starting to pop out. We finally dropped down and came into the area near Stillwater. By now things looked familiar to me, having been that way three times previously. Fresh bear and deer tracks were present all along the trail, giving evidence of bear feeding on the huckleberries. I was glad to be approaching camp and the security of the cabin and a fire. Finally the camp site came into view, and the horses picked up the pace, anticipating the offloading and a meal short at hand.

Once we had the horses secured, I worked at unloading and getting saddles and bridles off and hung up. Ted opened the cabin, got the fire going, and worked at stowing gear and provisions. I could see the water not far off, and a bit of a shiver went through me, anticipating the fishing and what it might hold in store. This was to be my last trip in, perhaps forever. I had no idea what the future held, so I savored every minute and took it all in.

As the afternoon and evening progressed, we took our supper of fresh grouse, cleaned up, built a campfire, and settled in for a bit of conversation. Ted related stories and observations of the trips over the years that Dad and Walt Kastner had taken—tales of game taken, the time they missed a bear, a trophy-size grizzly, Dad's moose, and of course, fish, including the one that hangs over the desk on which I'm writing this book. That fish is twenty-one inches and probably weighed close to four pounds. Ted said he caught it on a flatfish, and it took him forever to get it in.

I told Ted a bit about my home life, the family, and some of the disruption in my life. He encouraged me to continue to make good decisions and finish school. He was passionate about education, as would be reflected in his children as the years played out.

View of Stillwater from the cabin.

As the fired died, revealing only embers, he noted, "Ve need to get up early and see if ve can find the fish. I think it's going to be a good day."

Turning in and settling into my bunk padded with fir boughs, the events of the day and the whole summer came over me. The several months had been quite a ride, a time in my life not to be taken lightly. The events of that summer shaped a number of the corners of my life in years to come. I would reflect on this summer frequently, telling the stories and re-living the events. Sleep came on me heavily that night; I was physically and mentally tapped.

Ted didn't beat me to the stove the next morning. I had a fire going and coffee on before his feet hit the floor. That didn't mean he wasn't awake. He probably just wanted to see how badly I wanted that fish. The usual went forward that morning—eat a light breakfast, feed the horses, get water, and so on. Following the morning routine, we loaded the boat and headed up river. Passing the sandbar where he had shot the goose earlier in the summer and moving up stream further, we came to a place where the river widened and grass grew in the shallows. Ted moved in closer to the grass, and we anchored out of the current.

That area was flat on one side of the river. Cedar trees grew down to the water's edge, and dead standing trees remained in the water from when the river had been more of a channel. Trout loved to hide out in the stumps and forage further out in the river for food, thus making them available to the occasional eagle or, better still, us. We both fished that day, using spoons and spinners. We had really good luck in that spot as well as a couple of others. Later that day, I tied into a really big trout, over twenty inches, and probably four to five pounds. The excitement of the catch overcame me. I felt the emotions

In Pursuit of the GIANT TROUT

of victory over such a powerful fish and savored the moment. Ted netted the fish and brought it into the boat.

"It's a nice vun. Ve'll smoke it up, and you can take it home vith you."

With Ted's statements, I wondered if I'd caught *the* one. I asked, "Is this the knife fish?"

"No, no, no, ve haven't got that vun yet. Got to keep looking."

Now I thought it was beautiful and would gladly have given up the knife at that point, but he insisted that it was not *the* fish.

As the afternoon brought long streams of light through the trees and because our lunch was far gone, we gave up the hunt for the day. We had, by my count, caught every fish in that stretch of the river and released all but two for dinner and a nice big one for the smoker. It had been a beautiful day. We had spotted deer on the other side of the river, and a cow moose had moved along the edge of the backwater near shore. She hesitated several times, thinking about entering the water to feed, but our presence made her wary.

A strong spirituality holds sway in the forest, streams, and mountains. It takes over you and removes all sense of your origin, memory of the past, and thoughts of the future. You can focus only on the moment. Remaining in an awareness of this instant allows you to feel God's presence and gives you the ability to connect with him one-on-one. Many people speak of the experience of oneness with nature, but few understand that it provides the opportunity to walk and talk with God. I was one of those many at that age. I felt the experience but did not have the understanding to invite him in. That would come only many years later.

Returning to camp, we stowed the gear. Ted prepared the fish I had cleaned, and we hid the big trout in the river. Ted seemed to think we would add to it the next day with a couple more that size. I spent a bit of time going over my tackle, deciding which lures I would use tomorrow, wondering if I'd already caught the big fish or whether it still waited for me out there. Whether tomorrow brought one bigger or not, I would be happy; nothing could top this whole experience, and Ted would get his knife back, regardless. The fish was as big as or bigger than Dad's, for sure. A bigger fish would be nice, one that threatened to sink the boat or drag us downstream, but I was timid about pushing the issue. Ted, however, wanted one worthy of winning back his knife. Only a real giant would do—one that challenged the fishing skills of this city lad with the once uncalloused hands and the forever unbridled appetite!

Once again, we sat by the fire that night, talked of the history of the place, and pondered if natives had passed this way in the last few hundred years. Ted always revealed adventures he had been involved in, but I respected his sense of privacy on parts of his life and philosophy that he kept hidden. He was a man of many words and yet few.

Ted had a true passion for the woods, the hunting, fishing, and storytelling. He also had a distinct ability to rise to the occasion when his strength and voice needed to be called on. You always knew you had him on your side when things were going right, and he stayed with you when things went wrong, as long as you hadn't caused it! Either way, he never turned away from a situation that needed his help or involvement. Ted had said we'd find *the* one, and that sufficed. His confidence filled me, and we turned in early, planning on an early start in the morning.

Morning broke clear and cold that day. The fire soon had us warmed up, though, and we prepared to get out on the river. During the night, the horses had been restless, and Ted had gone out once to check on them. He'd seen nothing but suspected a bear.

I fed and watered them, and shortly after we shoved off. We traveled a little further up river in an area similar to the previous day. The crisp morning air cut at my cheeks and fingers, it was calm and the woods were still in shadows as the sun had not yet touched them.

We settled into a spot that showed promise. I cast out a number of times without results. Ted hooked and retrieved a nice trout, about the size of the one I had caught the day before, and we kept it. As the morning wore on and the sunlight lit up the surrounding woods, the clear brightness of the day seemed almost surreal. Ted decided to move back to where we had been the day before and fish the backwater a little closer in. We moved and anchored in the chosen spot. Ted had me remove my lure, and he got out a plain silver spoon. He pulled out a bottle of bright nail polish and painted two stripes on the spoon and blew on it.

"Let's try this and see if you can't coax in a big vun."

I cast my line out into the backwater and slowly retrieved the lure. The sun of summer lay lower on the water as each day passed. The leaves were starting to turn, and they gave off that aroma that fall was not far away. As I contemplated the changing season, Ted touched my shoulder, and I turned in his direction. He pointed to the grass on the edge of the backwater.

"Get ready. It's headed toward your lure."

I sped up the retrieve and watched as the fish headed in the direction of the lure. As it got closer, it picked up speed. At the moment of contact, a taste came in my mouth, like biting into a plugged-in lamp cord. The fish had a plan—scare the life out of me and see me fail in this duel of wits.

He got the first blow in. I was petrified.

The line immediately stripped off the reel; he headed for the stumps and logs where he knew I would snap him off. I applied a small amount of drag, and he slowed down in his quest to get to cover.

"Tip up, tip up!"

Ted had now entered the battle with verbal exchanges with the fish, some too colorful to write, but all encouraging my efforts. I gained a bit of line before he decided to turn direction and swim all the way across the backwater and head for the river. This smelled of disaster to me; he would have the current in his favor. I decided to test his strength and that of the line and hooking. I choked down on him, and he turned back. Now swimming faster than I could retrieve, he broke water on slack line and cleared his tail. This nearly stopped my heart. My first full look at the fish told me he would far surpass the previous day's effort. For what seemed hours, he explored the outer reaches of the backwater and returned to the boat, only to find renewed strength and go back out. I was growing fearful I would lose him, but Ted was sure he was jaw hooked. Finally after a long battle, the fish was losing his strength and slowly and reluctantly surrendered alongside the boat, allowing himself to be taken into the net.

At this point, Ted did not bring the net into the boat. Instead, we looked over the side and admired the fish's beauty and size. Ted measured the fish with several spans of his hand.

"It's about twenty-eight inches, probably eight or nine pounds."

Silence settled on the boat. I could not speak, for all the emotion I had encountered in my quest for this fish had come to the surface. All the thought and anticipation now lay in that net, and I didn't know what to do. Ted had found the place to tangle with a fish that put all my abilities to the test. I had never experienced that much strength and determination, such grace and poise, in something that gave every ounce of its being to the situation. It was a real battle of wits. In the end,

I won. I was the proven victor, conqueror of the waters around me, and yet I felt compassion for this fallen hero of battles past, a warrior to his comrades

Ted looked at me with compassion, understanding my internal dilemma. "Ve'll keep it if you vant, or ve can get a couple more to smoke for your trip home."

The fish, by now, had recovered some and showed signs of wanting another fight.

"I want to let it go. The knife is yours."

Ted took out a pair of cutters and surgically cut the hook and twisted it out of the jaw. I lowered the net below the surface, and the fish exploded out and raced towards the stumps and logs. Ted smiled, and looked me in the eye.

"I vant my dammed knife!" he shouted and grabbed my shoulder.

Tears kept my eyes from focusing. I felt relief that the ordeal of the giant trout was over. Peace and reflection could now close this chapter of my adventure.

The rest of the morning went equally well. We caught two more three-plus-pound fish, called it good, and headed back to Stillwater. We pulled the boat up and turned it over for Ted's next fishing party to enjoy. That afternoon, we prepared the fish. That night, we smoked them and stayed up late, making sure that the fish would be cured by the next morning when we would leave. This was our last night, the last time for me at the fire with Ted, the camp coffee, and the stories. I went to bed that night, knowing that it was mostly behind me, but it would never be wrestled from my memory. I slept soundly, and offered up a thank-you prayer, though I didn't truly have a connection to God yet. In my heart though, the Lord had touched me.

Morning came cold again, and the fire and hot coffee, as usual, gave great relief. We packed and moved our gear to the hitching post and retrieved the fish from the smokehouse. They were beautiful, bronzed and shiny from the alder smoke, and had a smell that only a fisherman can appreciate. We carefully wrapped them in newspaper to absorb the oil and packed them in the pack boxes. The horses showed a lot of excitement to get going and warm themselves up. Ted climbed into the saddle and grabbed the pack string. We took one last look at the Stillwater camp and were off. As we rode out through the lowland surrounding the camp, I reflected on my short hikes out from camp, the wood-gathering, berry-picking. It was all so beautiful.

The trip that day back to the farm went pretty much without event. Ranger and I both enjoyed the trip as he kept a steady pace and was a true gentleman. I would not ride another horse for twenty years, but the skills would all come back with the memory of how he had taught me to take charge and be a horseman.

Just about dusk, we made the last turn in the road and had the farmhouse in sight. The lights from the lanterns in the kitchen and dining room beckoned us, and Trixie and Fenris barked out a welcome. We pulled up to the hitching rail outside the front yard fence and tied up in the midst of welcomes and shrieking kids and a family once again together, as darkness descended on Hemp Creek.

The Journey Back Home

The next couple of days were a mix of activity. Several people stopped to say hi and good-bye. Of course, the immediate family, Roy and Marlene and the baby, and Ralph and Clara and their children, all bid me farewell. The Archibalds came by, and so did the Ludtkes. I was now having tugs of homesickness, mixed with thoughts of school, friends, and somewhere out there how I would tie this all up. The Two sensed that I would soon leave—their partner in adventure, swimming coach, bike-riding instructor, sword-builder, fishing partner, slave-master at the woodpile, rabbit-shooter, and most of all their friend. How would I ever be able to repay all that these people had contributed to this amazing summer—the adventure, trust, comfort, incredible food, and their friendship? Maybe if I took the time someday to write a book about it, I could share how much the summer meant to me.

I spent the last day or so finishing up the woodpile. It had grown out the doors of the shed and onto the front porch. I filled up the wood box in the kitchen and stacked some in the tack barn. I fished Hemp Creek one more time with Jim and Ellen. We had a little supper of fried trout that night and shared about the fly-versus-bait contests we had had.

Friday night arrived, my last at the farm on Hemp Creek. There was a family on vacation staying in the cabin Dad and I had occupied. They would be traveling back to New Westminster the next day and had offered me a ride to their home and would put me on the bus to Seattle in Vancouver on Sunday. I spent the evening packing the last of my gear in my duffle bag and a knapsack for my fishing gear. My two poles were in tubes, so would be protected; I was ready.

Jim, Ellen, and I slept upstairs in their bedroom that night. We talked and made promises about how we would stay in touch and write each other. The pull towards home was now becoming almost uncomfortable. I thought a lot about what I'd tell everyone about my summer and all the adventures. Sleep came late and finally filled the void with dreams, taking me back through the summer.

Saturday morning came, and the family all showed up for my last breakfast—Roy and Marlene, Clara and Ralph. Jennie had cooked up a meal to tide me over for several months: bacon, hotcakes, eggs, the big pitcher of fresh milk, coffee. Everyone had his fill. I brought the knife to breakfast and graciously presented it to Ted, which pleased him to no end.

He carefully examined it and noted, "It needs to be sharpened!"

Jim and Ellen stayed close to me the whole morning, hovering as if I might get away. I received many last minute comments about how much they had enjoyed my visit and hoped to hear from me when I returned home. Ted thanked me for all the hard work I had put in around the farm and especially the woodpile. He reached in his pocket and pulled out some folded bills.

"I told you I'd pay twenty-five dollars for the vood. You did a good job and more vood than I expected. Here's a little extra for all the hard vork. Thank you Paul!"

Fifty bucks! More money than I'd ever held in my hand up to then. A surprise ending to sore shoulders and blistered hands, I felt accomplished.

Shortly, the folks taking me back to their place came down the road in their station wagon and pulled up to the fence. The Two helped me carry my gear and a shopping bag full of smoked trout wrapped in newspaper. We all went out and met them and exchanged conversation as we loaded my gear into the car. The time had come to say our good-byes; I was having some trouble with that. The Two clung to my legs like orphans. Jennie gave me a warm hug and thanked me for all my help and time with The Two. Ted, slightly somber, eyes looking moister than normal but showing his usual composed and stalwart self, took my hand in a grip that threatened to shatter all my knuckles.

He touched my other shoulder and said, "Paul, it's been a pleasure having you here this summer. Come back vith your Dad anytime. Ve'll go shoot a moose!"

That was enough to tell me things had gone well between us, all and more than I could have prayed for. We separated, and I got into the back seat of the station wagon and rolled down the window. The people had two children as well, and we all got situated in the back.

The station wagon backed out and turned down the road towards Hemp Creek. I turned in my seat and quickly waved out the window at the family standing outside the fence by the hitching rail. On the other side of the road at the fence to the north pasture stood the herd and, of course, Ranger. I had said my good-byes to him earlier. He had seemed standoffish, as though he didn't want to deal with our impending separation. But now his head was erect, and he stood proudly by the fence. I would miss him also; he had been patient with my ineptness and taught me so much. Soon we were crossing the log bridge that spanned Hemp Creek. We slowed not for the view but to ease gently over a very bumpy bridge, which gave me a contemplative view of the meandering stream. Hemp Creek in the summer flowed slowly, a rich light cider color from the leaves and vegetation. Trout dashed and darted from hiding place to hiding place, constantly in search of bugs and such. The grasses and trees hung over the water, giving it serenity and yet a sense of curiosity.

I was now moving into another phase of the journey, as well as being quizzed by the good people I traveled with. They had stayed for two weeks, fished the creek, and done a bit of hiking. They were nice people, friendly and full of conversation. The two children visited with me about Jim and Ellen, my summer, and all the usual.

The trip down the gravel road to Clearwater took the next hour, a drive I had made several times in the pickup truck with Roy or Ted. As we approached town, the power poles appeared on the side of the road. I glanced up to see if Beeper, my traveling companion, was still sitting up there. I think he must have had a companion; he never looked down nor fired a glass insulator at the station wagon. He would become another boy's travel friend, and I would find someone else to share my adventures with in time.

We stopped in Kamloops for lunch, continued on to their home in New Westminster, east of Vancouver, British Columbia, and arrived there late in the evening. We pulled into their driveway and got out. The folks opened up the house while I opened the tailgate of the station wagon and started taking luggage and sleeping bags out. In the midst of this, some movement caught my eye. I looked in the back of the wagon, and there sat a mid-size mountain beaver that had just crawled out between the bags and luggage. Apparently he had crawled into one of the bags when the family was loading their gear back at their cabin. He looked as shocked as we did. We stepped back, and he lumbered to the edge and fell down to the ground and went to the side of the yard, disappearing into some brush. He had traveled a long way to take up residence in the suburbs. I don't think he was going to find it as hospitable as the park.

The parents set up an air mattress on the floor in their basement recreation room, and I slept in my bag that night. I felt very lost, still in transition between home and the farm. It seemed like years since I'd been at either. In the morning, we had a light breakfast and got back in the wagon and drove into Vancouver. There they helped me get a ticket, and I said farewell as I climbed on the bus to Seattle.

The bus was nearly full, and I was seated with a nice elderly lady, who seemed quite interested in my whereabouts and the contents of the shopping bag, which now smelled as if it was on fire. I obliged her by removing one of the smaller newspaper packages in the bag and opening it. She was a mix of shock, surprise, and curiosity as she gingerly took a small piece of the fish, which I had torn off, but showed pleasure at its delicate flavor and color. Two guys on the other side of the aisle got wind of what was taking place and insisted on trying it also. As the miles rolled on, the bus became engrossed in passing samples up and down the aisle; eventually even the driver got a piece. The sum of the event is that I got home with only two of the four fish, but I got to tell lots of stories to the passengers around me about the summer.

That afternoon, the bus pulled into the Seattle terminal. I called Dad, and he came down to the station and picked me up. He shook my hand and thumped my chest with the back of his hand, as was customary in our greetings. On the ride out to my mom's house, I shared with him the highlights of the summer and, of course, the giant trout. Dad was obviously pleased with the outcome of the summer. I would not know for years how much he wished that he had been Ted that summer, but circumstances forbade it at the time. Nevertheless, he appreciated all that Ted and the family experience had afforded me.

My mother greeted me at the door and cried a bit, so happy to have me home and safe. That night over dinner, I told her as much as I could of my summer, and she shared stories of her own at home.

Reflections

Mom suffered from a number of physical and mental health issues most of her adult life. I knew that her summer had not gone perfectly but was at a loss for what I, a mere fifteen-year-old, could do to help. We stayed together till the year of my seventeenth birthday, when she felt I would do better living with my dad. That was her way of letting me go slowly, as her health continued to fail. She died shortly after my eighteenth birthday. I experienced the loss as a chapter in my life closed and spent some time questioning its significance, not arriving at answers for years.

My father remarried a wonderful woman, Susie to all of us, who was very much a part of our family for the next forty years. She reminded me, early on, that she was not a replacement for my mother, that she was there only to fill a void in my dad's life and, of course, in mine if I asked. She was a true spirit and provided me answers to questions I had not been able to ask my mother. I loved her very much. She, also, was a mentor.

My sister, Sarah (Sally), married Frank Burgess, and they had three beautiful daughters. They all live in eastern Washington, where Sarah and Frank enjoy retirement.

My brother, Carl, married just out of the air force. They had one daughter and divorced shortly after. Soon after he retired in 1996, he died in a tragic fishing accident off Vancouver Island, British Columbia. I grieved the loss in that we were just getting to the subject of what had gone down between us over the years and had briefly talked about it the week before he passed away. I have forgiven him and am at peace with our relationship.

As the years rolled on, I graduated from high school, was drafted into the Army, served a tour in Vietnam, and returned home to meet Linda, the woman who would soon become my wife, lover, eventual fishing partner, and provide us with three sons. Today, she and I are mostly retired; the boys are grown and successful young men, and we have five grandchildren by our youngest son and his beautiful wife. They fill the air with the sounds of discovery, joy, praise, and adventure. They represent the next generation of adventurers and seekers of the Lord's word, continually asking questions and taking in the daily obstacles that appear before them. I see great promise in the future for our three sons. They continue to draw my admiration and respect. I only hope that I imparted some wisdom upon them, for that is my station in life as their father and mentor.

What happened at the Helsets represents some of the essentials I needed to continue my growth to manhood. I learned that each and every one of us needs a helping hand to grow in our circle of knowledge. We can get by on our own; however, the experiences may not be as well chosen as they would be by a mentor. My experiences of that summer, in addition to the times when others outside the family shared of themselves, has given me the knowledge that I am loved and the ability to extend that precious commodity of love and mentoring outside the family.

Reflections

Hemp Creek from the bridge
2006

I can't emphasize enough how truly important it is to take stock of what you have to offer to others. Listen to your heart; it knows what's within you and how to share it with those in need. Wonderful adventures await us all—we have fish to be caught, stories to be told, hearts to be spoken to, and an abundance of Dads, Ted Helsets, mentors of all ages and abilities. It is entrusted to us to make the connections for the sake of hearts yet to be touched.

Epilogue

Mentoring can happen any time, at any stage in one's life, with any person, and through any number of experiences. My story reflects but one among myriad possibilities.

Lost opportunities of mentoring can get another chance. Sometimes, our vision and hearing don't fully mature till we reach adulthood. I have met many a man who ended up going back to his father as an adult and bringing him to the understanding of what a son needs from a dad. Other men never get that opportunity to connect with their father but start fresh with their own sons.

Yet before even that relationship can develop, we must recognize the most basic father-son relationship—between God, our father, and us, his sons. He has been alongside us from the start, mentoring when we would listen, giving guidance, and helping us to choose our steps carefully.

I know. I speak from experience.

When did I receive this revelation about how important being a father to my sons is? The simple truth is not till I had accepted the fact that the Lord is really my true father. Yes, I was blessed with a man who watched over me, guided me, gave me real life adventures. But my father could not give me a knowledge of his presence from the moment of my birth and for the rest of my life. Only God can. And this awareness did not become clear to me till I accepted Christ as my personal Lord and Savior at the age of sixty.

I have three sons, and I fumbled along in their upbringing without understanding that first father-son relationship. I realize that, without it, I tried too hard with the first son, questioned myself and my abilities with the second, and backed off on the third. So, each of the boys got a different experience in fathering, reflected in their different personalities and chosen paths in life.

We belong to Adventure Community Church in Duvall, Washington, with a very intimate population of just over three hundred. It has a men's group that meets on Wednesday nights, and on regular occasions, draws between fifty and seventy-five men. That's close to 25 percent of the church population. Most of the men attend with the same focus level as if they're watching a sports broadcast. (You've noticed that we don't meet on Monday night!) The topic of discussion? Connecting a man's heart to the Lord and dealing with the wounds that heart still carries.

Our scars affect how we conduct ourselves and directly impact our ability to mentor our boys. Healing and forgiving the neglect of mentoring or any abuse far beyond that allows a better relationship to develop between us and our own sons, as well as between us and our fathers.

Fathers, focus on what it means to a son for you just to be there, even if other parts of the equation have been lost. As long as you nurture the ability of a son to hear your love for him, he will watch you, take knowledge from you, grow

Epilogue

from the experiences you offer him, and give you the greatest reward—he will take all that on to the next generation.

Men, fathers and sons, go forward from wherever you stand today and focus on what you already are doing right. Share that with other men who so desperately need direction and the knowledge that they are not alone. Share your mentoring skills with young boys and young men who are not able to get it from their own father.

Fathers, as you awaken to a deficiency in your relationship with your sons, be patient. Reach out and accept help. Look to resources for guidance in establishing a more satisfying father-son relationship.

Remember, too, that time constraints vary over the lifetime of a marriage. You may have to be absent more often during one period, so you must focus on those short times you do have, in the morning and evening, perhaps, to give your son what he needs—his dad's attention connected to mentoring through action or praise. You will find that you can make more free time in the relationship as time goes by—and you will want to because of the joy you take in being with your son. Remember, the gift is not how many trips you take or how many toys you give; it is the genuine message you convey to him of how much you love him, that you want to be a part of his life, and that you are there to help him develop into a man of good character.

I lost contact with those wonderful people for nearly fifty years. When the book idea started to manifest itself, the feelings in my heart directed me to reach out and renew some of those contacts. The years between that summer and when I started this project were taken up with school, the military, and raising a family, with little time spent reflecting. I first made contact with Roy Helset. As I started introducing myself

Remains of farm house
2006

Helset family
(Left to Right) Jim Clara Roy Ellen and Harold

on the phone, he cut me off. "Paul, it's so good to hear your voice. Let me finish that story for you. We thought maybe you had died in Vietnam, wondered why we never heard back from you."

I then contacted The Two: Jim, who lives on Salt Spring Island, British Columbia with his wife Carol, and Ellen, who still lives in the Clearwater area. Later that summer in 2006, Linda and I drove up to Clearwater, British Columbia, and met with Jim and Ellen at the home she shares with her husband, Kelly, which is where Ted and Jennie lived out the last years of their lives. We traveled about fifteen miles north to the site of the farm, now abandoned, and reminisced as we wandered through what was left of the place. Jim and Ellen have been a great source of strength and helped fill in some of the details which had eluded my memory.

John Eldredge with Ransomed Heart Ministries (www.ransomedheart.com) has a number of books on the subject of mentoring. An incredibly talented man, he discovered his wounded heart and now shares his knowledge, vision, and understanding of our connection to the Lord with thousands of men so that their healing can begin.

Farmhouse
2006

If

By Rudyard Kipling

If you can keep your head when all about you
Are losing theirs and blaming it on you;
If you can trust yourself when all men doubt you,
But make allowance for their doubting too;
If you can wait and not be tired by waiting,
Or, being lied about, don't deal in lies,
Or, being hated, don't give way to hating,
And yet don't look too good, nor talk too wise;

If you can dream—and not make dreams your master;
If you can think—and not make thoughts your aim;
If you can meet with triumph and disaster
And treat those two imposters just the same;
If you can bear to hear the truth you've spoken
Twisted by knaves to make a trap for fools,
Or watch the things you gave your life to broken,
And stoop and build 'em up with worn out tools;

If you can make one heap of all your winnings
And risk it on one turn of pitch-and-toss,
And lose, and start again at your beginnings

And never breath a word about your loss;
If you can force your heart and nerve and sinew
To serve your turn long after they are gone,
And so hold on when there is nothing in you
Except the Will which says to them: "Hold on";

If you can talk with crowds and keep your virtue,
Or walk with kings—nor lose the common touch;
If neither foes nor loving friends can hurt you;
If all men count with you, but none too much;
If you can fill the unforgiving minute
With sixty seconds' worth of distance run—
Yours is the Earth and everything that's in it,
And—which is more—you'll be a Man my son!